BARRON'S DOG BIBLES

Australian Shepherds

D. Caroline Coile, Ph.D.

BARRON'S

Acknowledgments

I am deeply indebted to C. A. Sharp of the Australian Shepherd Health and Genetics Institute, who is a font of information not only about health and genetics, but basically everything Aussie.

About the Author

D. Caroline Coile, Ph.D., has written 35 books and more than 500 magazine and scientific articles about dogs—and one book about cats. She's also a columnist for *Dog World* magazine and the *AKC Gazette.* Her dog writing awards include the Dog Writer's Association of America Maxwell Award (eight times), the Denlinger Award, the Eukanuba Canine Health Award (twice), and the AKC Canine Health Foundation Award (twice). She is the author of the top-selling *Barron's Encyclopedia of Dog Breeds.* Caroline's research and teaching interests revolve around canine behavior, senses, and genetics. On a practical level, Caroline has lived with dogs all of her life and competed with them for more than 35 years. Her dogs have included nationally ranked show, field, obedience, and agility competitors, with Best in Show, Best in Field, and High in Trial (in both obedience and agility) awards.

> All information and advice contained in this book has been reviewed by a veterinarian.

A Word About Pronouns

Many dog lovers feel that the pronoun "it" is not appropriate when referring to a pet that can be such a wonderful part of our lives. For this reason, Australian Shepherds are described as "he" throughout this book unless the topic specifically relates to female dogs. This by no means infers any preference, nor should it be taken as an indication that either sex is particularly problematic.

Cover Credits

Front cover: Shutterstock
Back cover: Tara Darling

Photo Credits

Seth Casteel: pages 8, 34, 39, 46, 59, 60, 85, 112, 114, 150; Kent Dannen: pages 2, 133; Cheryl Ertelt: pages 94, 130, 153; Shirley Fernandez: pages 24, 63; Sharon Eide Elizabeth Flynn: pages vi, 6, 80, 154, 159; jeanmfogle.com: pages 12, 41, 71, 86, 106, 116, 118, 121, 129, 147, 149; Daniel Johnson: pages 82, 97, 120, 136 (top, bottom), 137 (top, bottom), 138 (top, bottom), 139 (top, bottom), 140 (top, bottom), 141 (top, bottom), 142; Paulette Johnson: pages 14, 18, 20, 44, 50, 53, 55, 61, 72, 74, 89, 103, 144; Lisa Kruss: pages 56, 66; Paws on the Run: pages v, 11, 48, 58, 79, 156, 164, 166; Shutterstock: pages i, iii, 22, 26, 28, 33, 123, 170; SmartPakCanine.com: pages 37, 162; Steve Surfman: page 81.

All inquiries should be addressed to:
Barron's Educational Series, Inc.
250 Wireless Boulevard
Hauppauge, New York 11788
www.barronseduc.com

ISBN: 978-0-7641-4551-3 (Book)
ISBN: 978-0-7641-8678-3 (DVD)
ISBN: 978-1-4380-7016-2 (Package)

Library of Congress Catalog Card No: 2010027878

Library of Congress Cataloging-in-Publication Data
Coile, D. Caroline.
   Australian shepherds / by D. Caroline Coile.
      p. cm. — (Barron's dog bibles)
   Includes index.
   ISBN-13: 978-0-7641-4551-3
   ISBN-10: 0-7641-4551-7
   ISBN-13: 978-0-7641-8678-3
   ISBN-10: 0-7641-8678-7
   1. Australian shepherd dog. I. Title.
   SF429.A79C65 2011
   636.737—dc22   2010027878

Printed in China

9 8 7 6 5 4 3

CONTENTS

CONTENTS

The Australian Shepherd is an overachiever. Energetic herder, hop-to-it obedience worker, all-around ranch dog, diligent guardian, and always-by-your-side companion—that's the Aussie. And that's why Aussies have steadily risen in popularity as more people discover this versatile, all-American (yes, American) breed. But, it's also why the Aussie's numbers have risen in rescue; not everyone can keep up with a dog who's not content to lounge inside all day or be banished to a life alone in the backyard. Active Aussies need active lifestyles.

This is your invitation to learn whether the Aussie is the dog for you, and if so, to discover ways to enjoy and care for your Aussie. In this book, you'll learn about the Aussie's interesting (if obscure) history; what makes him tick; how to find a good one (and that includes rescue options); the difference between American Kennel Club (AKC) and Australian Shepherd Club of America (ASCA) registration; how to feed and groom your Aussie; special medical concerns (including some special drug precautions peculiar to some Aussies); and how to train your Aussie for both competitions and companionship.

The Aussie has come a long way from its working roots background, but this breed will work its hardest to please you no matter what you ask. All the Aussie asks for in return is that you understand him, care for him, and treat him fairly. And that's the goal of this book.

Chapter One

All About Australian Shepherds

Here's the short history of the Australian Shepherd: Nobody knows where they're from.

But breed historians do have theories. All agree that herding dogs were developed thousands of years ago, probably in Europe in pre-Roman times. After that, agreement ends.

Australian Shepherd Beginnings

The Basque people, who were known by ancient Roman times, are usually credited with the early development of many herding dogs in the region of northeastern Spain and southwestern France around the western end of the Pyrenees. But other European cultures also developed strains of sheepherding dogs. Any of these dogs could have been brought to both America and Australia in the 1800s.

Immigrant farmers to Australia included the Scots, who would have brought their Scottish Collie; the English, who would have brought several types of stockdogs, including the Smithfield and Dorset Blue Shag (both of which were often docked close); the Welsh, who would have brought the Welsh Gray Sheepdog and the Welsh Blue-Grey; the Irish, who would have brought their Glenwherry Collies; and the Germans, who would have brought their Wallis Sheepdogs. When Merino sheep from Spain became popular in Australia in the 1800s, Basque shepherds, along with their Pyrenees Sheepdogs and Catalan Sheepdogs, emigrated to Australia to work them. The various strains of stockdogs would have eventually been interbred, with emphasis on creating dogs that could work sheep in the harsh Australian land. Some of the strains they developed were the German Coulie, Huntaway, Kelpie, and Smithfield Collie.

A similar mix of immigrant farmers and stockdogs, along with Merino sheep, came from Europe to America at about the same time. Eventually, sheep, farmers, and stockdogs, including some of the newly developed strains or crosses, came to America from Australia as well.

By the late 1920s, the name "Australian Shepherd" appears to have been in use in several parts of the western United States to identify many of these stockdogs, particularly those that arrived from Australia. The name probably seemed somewhat exotic and charismatic, and owners didn't shy from using it simply because the dogs weren't actually a breed and in fact were likely recent crosses. No attempt was made to create a pure breed, as emphasis was on working ability rather than appearance or pedigree.

In the 1940s, thousands of Basque sheepherders were actively recruited to work sheep in the western United States (particularly Idaho, Colorado, and the Pacific Northwest) as there was a shortage of labor during World War II. Many of them brought their trained "little blue dogs" with them. These dogs were probably Pyrenees Sheepdogs (also known as Bergers de Pyrenees). It is possible that these dogs contributed to the strain already dubbed the Australian Shepherd.

So which is the true Australian Shepherd ancestor? Good arguments can be made for several breeds, particularly the Pyrenees Sheepdog from Spain, the German Coulie of Australia, and to a lesser extent, the Old Welsh Bobtail from Wales. The breeds share many of the same physical and working characteristics, and all were in the right place at the right time to have contributed to the Aussie gene pool. In addition, a strong argument has been made for the contribution of the Smithfield, once common in Australia but now found mostly in Tazmania, as an important ancestor. Finally, existing sheepdogs in America, most of which came from European stock generations earlier, doubtless contributed to the mix. As these breeds are themselves all interrelated, the chances are that the Aussie, like all true Americans, is the result of a melting pot of breeds and strains.

Jay Sisler and the Rodeo Show

The Australian Shepherd continued to prosper in the West, proving itself an invaluable ranch hand. These dogs had to be quick, hardy, obedient, intelligent, weatherproof, and tireless. Generations of selection for working ability produced the American West's preeminent sheepdog, yet it was still more of a strain or type than a breed. The dogs were relatively unknown outside of the west or off the ranch. That situation changed with a man named Jay Sisler.

Sisler obtained his first "blue dog" around 1939 and trained his first ones around 1949. These two dogs, Stub and Shorty, learned to spin and dance, feign a hurt leg, jump rope, and ride a teeter-totter, among other tricks. He took his trick dog show on the rodeo circuit, eventually adding other dogs and tricks to the act. By the 1960s he was traveling more than 750,000 miles a year and performing at such places and events as the Calgary Stampede, Seattle World's Fair, and Madison Square Garden. His dogs also appeared in movies, most notably *Run Appaloosa Run* and *Stub: The Best Cow Dog in the West*. The latter was the story of three Australian "cow cutter" shepherd dogs named Stub, Queen, and Shorty. More than anyone, Sisler popularized the Australian Shepherd through exposure in rodeo shows and movies. Although he never considered himself a breeder, he bred many litters and placed his puppies throughout the West, particularly in the northwestern United States and Canada.

Recognition

Even before the Aussie found fame on the big screen, a few dog fanciers, mostly in the western United States, had discovered these impressive dogs. In 1957, they formed the Australian Shepherd Club of America (ASCA). In that same year the National Stock Dog Registry (NSDR) became the official registration body for the breed. The NSDR's influence continued to help ensure that the Aussie would remain a functional herding dog rather than a dog bred primarily for beauty. As the breed gained in popularity, however, more fanciers also wanted to enjoy competition in obedience and conformation forums, and in 1971 the ASCA took over as the official registry. Aussies registered with the ASCA could partake in a wide variety of competitive venues, making the Aussie more attractive to fanciers who were not in a position to train their dogs for stockdog trials. Now the Aussie could make its mark in conformation, obedience, tracking, and herding.

Breed Truths

Registration Numbers

You can tell if a dog is AKC or ASCA registered by his registration number. AKC numbers start with the letters DL or DN, followed by eight numbers. ASCA numbers start with the letter E and are followed by six numbers.

In 1977 a breed standard by which the conformation of Aussies could be objectively evaluated was approved. For some Aussie fanciers, the next logical step was to seek American Kennel Club (AKC) recognition. Not all Aussie fanciers wanted AKC recognition, however, so when it was proposed in 1985 the ASCA declined to pursue AKC affiliation. Many club members feared that the emphasis on conformation competition that often accompanies AKC recognition would divide the breed into show and working types, rather than the all-purpose Aussie they valued. In addition, the increased popularity that is sometimes created by the words "AKC registered" was worrisome, as the Aussie was not a breed for everyone. Several Aussie breeders nonetheless felt that AKC recognition would benefit the breed, and they formed the United States Australian Shepherd Association (USASA) in 1991. They modified the ASCA standard and petitioned the AKC for full recognition, which was granted in 1993.

The situation has left the Australian Shepherd with two parent clubs in the United States: The original and largest is the ASCA, whereas the official AKC club is the USASA. So strongly did some Aussie breeders object to AKC recognition that they declined the invitation to register their stock with the AKC. Despite these differences of opinion, a number of Aussie breeders supported the opportunity for AKC recognition and registered their stock with both registries. The Aussie has since become a major contender in the Herding group at AKC dog shows and a strong competitor at AKC obedience, agility, and herding trials. It is still a valued working dog and staunch stockdog contender at non-AKC stockdog (herding) trials. Despite an influx of fanciers interested primarily in show, the Aussie has kept a base of breeders who believe it should be above all a working stockdog with exceptional temperament.

The Aussie has continued to grow in popularity as a pet, but not always for the good of the dogs, their owners, or the breed as a whole. Although the breed seems to have withstood many of the detrimental aspects of AKC recognition, its increased popularity has left many people unprepared for the Aussie's need for mental and physical stimulation with a dog they cannot

FYI: Non-standard Coat Colors

As the Australian Shepherd is a recently developed breed—and one that until comparatively recent years was bred for function first, with aesthetics and purity of pedigree of lesser importance—it should not be surprising that nontraditional coat colors and patterns are still in the breed's gene pool and occasionally crop up in litters. While these colors are not acceptable from the point of view of the breed standard, they are nonetheless often eye-catching and do not adversely affect health, temperament, or working ability. They should not, however, be thought of as valuable because they are rare; they are rare because responsible breeders try not to perpetuate them.

Dilute coloration is one example. The dilution gene is recessive, so both parents must carry it. Dilute dogs cannot form fully saturated pigmented areas on the body, although tan- or copper-pointed dogs can form saturated copper on the trim. Dilute black areas become slate gray, and gray areas become silvery. Brown areas become silvery-brown or silvery-cream. Don't confuse the gray or silver areas of blue merles with dilution; if just one patch of saturated black hair is present, the dog is not dilute. Red merles can be more difficult to differentiate from dilute reds, as dilutes may simply appear to be washed-out reds. Some Aussies have dilute spots, which should not be confused with full dilution.

An unrelated type of dilution is caused by a recessive gene that produces gold or "peach," as some Aussie breeders call it. Two copies of this gene result in all black and brown hair being blocked, so dogs are some shade of yellow, from rich yellow to gold.

Other color patterns very occasionally seen in Aussies are sable (like the body color commonly seen in Lassie-colored Collies), saddle (like the black saddle on Rin-Tin-Tin-colored German Shepherds), or brindle (irregular vertical dark stripes overlying a lighter base color). Aussies with excessive white may be caused by merle-to-merle breedings but can also arise from overextended white trim. The genes that cause this are totally unrelated to the merle gene, and they do not cause the same health problems. However, because it's hard to tell if a merle with excessive white is actually a double merle or simply one with overly extensive white trim, the breed standard prohibits excessive white no matter what the cause.

handle, and which they ultimately turn over to rescue. Overall, however, the Aussie has benefited from having two strong breed clubs both working toward its well-being and the education of future owners.

Australian Shepherd Choices

One appealing characteristic of Aussies is that they aren't a cookie-cutter breed. They come in a range of sizes, colors, patterns, eye colors, and even tail length.

Coat Color Aussies come in two base colors: black and red. These can be merle or non-merle, and may also include a variety of white and tan markings on the face, chest, and legs. Taken together, these choices make for an overwhelming array of colors and patterns. There's nothing to recommend one color over another except for your personal preference. You should, however, avoid Aussies that are predominantly white if both parents are merles (see page 27). The merle pattern, which consists of irregular patches of dark fur interspersed over lighter fur, is caused by the action of one dominant gene. When two merles are bred together, they can produce puppies with two of these genes, which causes large areas of white fur in addition to the merle patterning, along with a high chance of auditory and visual problems. But because white trim is normal in Aussies, and is caused by a separate gene not related to the merle gene, it's possible that an Aussie with a lot of white is perfectly normal, especially if his parents are not both merles.

Eye Color The eyes also come in a variety of colors—and may not even match! In fact, each eye can be a combination of colors. Possible eye colors are glassy blue, amber, hazel, and all shades of brown. Blue eyes are most often associated with the merle coat pattern, but they can also appear in non-merle dogs. Blue eyes in non-merles are believed to be caused by a different gene than are blue eyes in merles. Aussies see just as well out of blue eyes as any other color, although the light eyes are probably a little more sensitive to bright light, just as blue eyes in people are slightly more sensitive.

Tail Length In North America it is customary to dock Aussie tails within a few days of birth. There's no medical reason for the procedure, and

if you'd rather have an Aussie with a long tail, you may be able to request that the puppy of your choice remain undocked. The breeder may not agree, however, because if you change your mind the puppy may be more difficult to place. Some Aussies are born with a natural bob or short tail. This trait tends to run in families, as the gene that causes bobtails is a dominant one. In fact, dogs with two copies of this gene usually die as embryos. If you favor the bobtail look but don't like the idea of docking, you may be able to find a family that has natural bobtails. If you've never seen an Aussie with a long tail, go to *www.youtube.com* and search for "Australian Shepherd long tail."

The Australian Shepherd Today

Today Australian Shepherds are the 28th (out of 164) most popular breed per AKC registrations. This doesn't count the Aussies that are only registered with the ASCA, so it's safe to say that Aussies are one of the top 25 breeds in America. During the last few years they have moved up in AKC popularity slowly but steadily.

Aussies are still used as stockdogs on many farms, but they are more often seen as suburban companions and competitive obedience and agility dogs. Their medium size, high intelligence, and good looks have made them a favorite of people looking for a family dog or fun-loving partner. While the Aussie's good looks help turn heads and gain admirers, there's no doubt that Aussie lovers are most enamored of the breed's do-it-all attitude. Lively, obedient, intelligent, courageous, and loyal, the Aussie has a "What's next?" attitude toward life. If you're a person who also likes to get going, the Aussie may be the dog to get going with.

Breed Truths

Miniature Australian Shepherds

Australian Shepherds are medium-sized dogs, but miniature Australian Shepherds are small or even toy-sized. More properly called North American Shepherds, North American Miniature Australian Shepherds, or Toy Australian Shepherds, these small Aussies are not recognized as a breed or as a variety of Australian Shepherd by either the ASCA or the AKC at this time. The ASCA will not accept them for registration, and the AKC will accept them only as standard Australian Shepherds (if both parents are registered Australian Shepherds). They can be registered with the North American Miniature Australian Shepherd Club of the USA (*www.namascusa.com*) or with the Miniature Australian Shepherd Club of America (*www.mascaonline.net*). The United Kennel Club recognizes them as a separate breed, the North American Shepherd. The AKC is in the process of bringing them into its Foundation Stock Service program, which is a preliminary step before possible recognition. If they do become AKC recognized, it will be under a name that does not contain "Australian Shepherd," and they will not be considered a variety of Australian Shepherd, but rather a separate breed.

Chapter Two

The Mind of the Australian Shepherd

Most Australian Shepherds today live as companions. But the breed was selected for working ability. Temperament is so integral to the breed's essence that it is described in the breed standards:

"The Australian Shepherd is intelligent, primarily a working dog of strong herding and guardian instincts. He is an exceptional companion. He is versatile and easily trained, performing his assigned tasks with great style and enthusiasm. He is reserved with strangers but does not exhibit shyness. Although an aggressive, authoritative worker, viciousness toward people or animals is intolerable." —from the Australian Shepherd Club of America breed standard.

"The Australian Shepherd is an intelligent working dog of strong herding and guarding instincts. He is a loyal companion and has the stamina to work all day . . . The Australian Shepherd is an intelligent, active dog with an even disposition; he is good natured, seldom quarrelsome. He may be somewhat reserved in initial meetings. Faults: Any display of shyness, fear, or aggression is to be severely penalized." —from the United States Australian Shepherd Association (AKC) breed standard.

The standards emphasize the breed's working ability, intelligence, guarding instinct, stamina, energy, and reserved nature with strangers. So what does this mean for a prospective owner?

Aussies and Energy

Dreaming of a dog to sit at your feet while you browse the Internet? A dog that can cuddle next to you on the couch while you watch television? An Aussie *can* be that dog—but not all day long, and only if he's also a dog that catches a Frisbee, goes on a hike, or practices some dog sport at some other point in the day.

Herding

When it comes to activity levels, herding breeds, like Australian Shepherds, tend to be near the top of the list. A dog expected to fetch a herd of sheep at the slightest notice, and keep them going in the direction they need to be

FYI: Australian Shepherd Pros and Cons

- If you don't like exercise . . .
- If you don't like a whirlwind of activity around you . . .
- If you don't like expectant eyes upon you whenever you put on shoes or pick up keys . . .
- If you get irritated by toys shoved in your lap all the time . . .
- If you don't want your arm to go numb from throwing . . .
- If you don't like company in the bathroom . . .
- If you don't like being firm . . .
- If you don't like dogs in your house . . .
- If you don't like hair on your floors . . .
- If you can't stand barking, even for a good reason . . .
- If you expect your dog to love everyone he meets . . .

Don't get an Aussie!
But . . .

- If you want a dog that's also your best friend . . .
- If you want a dog that's up for fun any time you are . . .
- If you want a dog that's protective without being aggressive . . .
- If you want a dog that's easy to please and always sees the bright side of life . . .
- If you want a dog that thinks helping you is fun . . .
- If you want a dog that's a good and trustworthy companion for your kids . . .
- If you want a dog that gets along well with others, including cats and other pets . . .
- If you want a dog that's cuddly but not clingy . . .
- If you want a dog to spend time outdoors with . . .
- If you want a hiking companion . . .
- If you want a versatile dog that you can compete with in many types of canine competitions . . .
- If you want a dog that's not high maintenance . . .

Then get an Aussie!

going, has to be ready to go at all times and prepared to keep on going for long periods. That's an Aussie. In fact, the Aussie's herding style, which is called upright and loose-eyed, requires more activity on the part of the dog. An upright herding dog means one that doesn't crouch; a loose-eyed dog means one that doesn't stare. Because crouching and staring are what predators do, sheep respond easily to such dogs (for example, Border Collies). Instead, Aussies must bounce and charge and bark to get the sheep to mind, all behaviors that take extra energy. Don't be surprised if your Aussie bounces and barks as part of his play—and if he seems like he could play forever.

Herding requires not only great physical energy but mental energy as well. A herding dog must be alert to his handler's commands and also to the sheep's movements, and be able to respond instantly and to think on his own. Even an Aussie who gets to go running every day may not be entirely fulfilled unless he also has a chance to flex his mental muscles. Training for herding, obedience, agility, or other mentally challenging activities will make your Aussie calmer and better behaved.

Aussies have a strong work ethic. They don't appreciate being unemployed. Their top career choice is herding, but they can also be satisfied with almost any job that takes mental or physical effort—and preferably both. If you don't give them a job, they may come up with their own job description, such as home redecorating, hole digging, barking, or just chasing their tails.

Exercise Needs

How much exercise is enough? Individual needs will vary. As stated, dogs from working lines tend to need more exercise than those from non-working lines. Younger dogs (except for young puppies) tend to need more exercise than older dogs. But be forewarned: Many Aussies are still out there herding in their teen years, so their energy level never gets really low. Males and females need about the same level of exercise.

In general, a walk is not enough. Even if the walk is a couple of miles, the typical Aussie will consider it a warm-up. A couple of miles running beside a bicycle, on the other hand, will usually suffice, and a jog of a couple of miles possibly will—although chances are he'll still want more. A good run three times a week is not enough; it needs to happen every day. Twenty

minutes of Frisbee catching is not enough. Its better to use fetch games as a supplement to other activities. Ten minutes of training is not enough; Aussies like to learn, and they can pay attention longer than many other breeds. Make it a couple of 30-minute sessions a day—even more, if you can. And that's in addition to the physical exercise.

High-Energy Housedogs

Aussies are able to turn off their herding mode when it comes time to be a family dog—as long as they have had some outlet for their mental and physical energy. Otherwise they may be "busy" housedogs, getting into the trash, chewing through a pants pocket, or just careening off the furniture.

Far too many Aussies can be found in shelters and rescue. And by far the top reason given by their former owners for giving them up is that they simply have too much energy. They've become hyperactive, and destructive, and in some cases made living with them unbearable. When adopted by a family with a matching energy level, these dogs blossom.

BE PREPARED! Be Honest

Before you get an Aussie at all, or one from working lines in particular, really think about your activity level. This means your true level—not how active you were with your last puppy 15 years ago, and not how active you think you'd be if only you had an active dog. It's sort of like buying jeans three sizes too small because you used to fit in them or you think they'll motivate you to losing weight. It doesn't work.

People tend to think admitting they aren't up to a high-energy dog is an admission that they're lazy, and tend to overestimate the activity level they can handle. Don't fall into this trap.

Although obedient by nature, Aussies are also active and herders by nature, which means fences and leashes are essential. While not wanderers, they can be chasers and may chase cars, kids on bicycles, cats, and other dogs. If you live near stock such as sheep or cattle, don't be surprised to find they've slipped through the fence and are trying to teach themselves to herd. This is seldom appreciated by people who own the stock.

Working Lines

It should come as no surprise that Aussies from working herding lines tend to be more active than those bred for companion or show purposes. This can be a problem; the typical new owner is entranced by the idea of owning a dog than can do what it was bred to do. It's a bragging point to say your dog's parents are working ranch dogs, handling flocks of sheep or perhaps an unruly steer. It's heady to look at a pedigree full of dogs with top herding titles. After all, isn't the point of breeding purebred dogs to create dogs that excel at what they were bred to do? Yes, it is—as long as you do your part and provide them with a ranch and a flock of sheep and the chance to work them. Otherwise it's like owning a Ferrari and only driving it up and down the driveway. Nobody is going to be happy.

Aussies and Intelligence

Aussies are overachievers. They can accomplish more in one day than most dogs can in a lifetime. Whether it's competing in an obedience trial, agility trial, or Flyball trial, or working as a herding dog, therapy dog, or search and rescue dog, the typical Aussie will always do his best to please you and excel—and he will usually succeed! Typically, you can be assured that Aussies will be among the top scorers at any event requiring obedience. They may not be at the very top in each category, but their versatility makes up for it.

The Aussie's obedience stems from his herding background. A herding dog must be able to follow a shepherd's commands instantly, and from a distance, even when they are contrary to what the dog wants to do. This doesn't mean Aussies come self-trained, however; you must still put in the time and effort to teach them, just as you would any smart and willing pupil.

People watching Aussies compete are naturally drawn to what appears to be a breed of canine Einsteins, but genius is not always an easy thing to live with. An intelligent child who is given no direction or stimulation is on the way to becoming a problem child; the same is true for an intelligent dog. If you plan to keep your Aussie in a crate for a good part of the day, or locked in the house alone while you work, you don't want a dog whose mind is racing with ideas and who needs entertainment. A dog can't read a book or watch TV when things are slow—it needs things to do. A smart dog will look for ways to entertain himself, and he will find them. A bored dog will dig, bark, get into the garbage, and chew. Then what happens? His owner tries to remove all the items with which the dog could entertain himself, or locks the dog in a crate or pen. Although Aussies may resign themselves to being quiet, when released they may be even more active, to the point the owner decides the dog is hyperactive.

Aussies are problem solvers, which can make life with them both more entertaining and more challenging. A fence may be seen as an obstacle you've placed there just to see how long it takes him to get to the other side. Placing food in the oven for safekeeping may be seen as an invitation to practice some safe-cracking. Repeating an obedience exercise he already knows may be seen as a chance to show you the other fifty ways it could be done. Add in the Aussie sense of humor, and life with an Aussie is never boring!

COMPATIBILITY Is an Aussie the Best Breed for You?

	Rating
ENERGY LEVEL	● ● ● ●
EXERCISE REQUIREMENTS	● ● ● ● ●
PLAYFULNESS	● ● ● ● ●
AFFECTION LEVEL	● ● ● ●
FRIENDLINESS TOWARD DOGS	● ● ●
FRIENDLINESS TOWARD PETS	● ● ●
FRIENDLINESS TOWARD STRANGERS	● ●
FRIENDLINESS TOWARD CHILDREN	● ● ● ●
INTELLIGENCE	● ● ● ● ●
EASE OF TRAINING	● ● ● ● ●
BARKING	● ● ● ●
DIGGING	● ●
CHEWING	● ● ●
WATCHDOG ABILITY	● ● ● ● ●
PROTECTION ABILITY	● ● ● ●
GROOMING REQUIREMENT	● ● ●
SHEDDING	● ● ●
COLOR CHOICES	● ● ● ●
COLD TOLERANCE	● ● ●
HEAT TOLERANCE	● ● ●
SPACE REQUIREMENTS	● ● ● ●
OK FOR BEGINNERS	● ● ● ●
HEALTHINESS	● ● ● ●
LIFE SPAN	● ● ● ●
PURCHASE PRICE	● ● ●
UPKEEP EXPENSE	● ● ●

5 Dots = Highest rating on scale

You need to exercise your Australian Shepherd's mind as well as his body. Training your dog not only tires out his brain but, with an Australian Shepherd, actually results in a well-mannered and obedient dog. For some breeds, training is a nice option; for Aussies, it is a necessity. They are too smart, too strong, and too active to remain without a leader. If you don't plan to lead, they will gladly take over.

BE PREPARED! What an Australian Shepherd Will Cost

Purchase: $250–$1000 ($50–$250 for a dog from a shelter or rescue group).

Spaying or neutering: $75–$250. Spaying costs more than neutering, and both cost more for larger dogs. Some communities offer low-cost spay-neuter clinics.

Vaccinations: $25–$75 per visit, with three visits typical in the first year. Some cities have low-cost clinics that provide basic services such as vaccinations at a lower fee.

Worming: $20–$30 per episode. Most puppies need to be wormed several times. Worming medications are dosed by weight, and tapeworm medication is the most expensive. Adults tend to need worming less often than puppies.

Heartworm prevention: $6–$8 per month. In most parts of the country, you'll need to start your puppy on heartworm prevention. The preventive is given once a month.

Flea prevention: $8–$15 per month. In most parts of the country, you'll need to start flea prevention right away. Prevention is cheaper than trying to rid your home of fleas.

Accidents and illnesses: $100–$200 and up for each minor illness or accident. Serious problems may cost hundreds to thousands of dollars. Pet health insurance is available (see page 87). Senior dogs often develop diseases that need ongoing treatment and entail high costs.

Food: $15–$35 per month. Dry food costs less than canned food.

Accessories: $20–$100. Collars, leashes, toys, crates, and dog beds should be included in your budget.

Boarding: $15–$40 per day. Rates are higher in metropolitan areas. Additional services, such as grooming, walking, or training, cost extra.

Obedience classes: $50–$150 per 8-week session. Private lessons cost more, while lessons offered by a dog or obedience club usually cost less.

Grooming: $40–$100 per month. Cut costs by having your veterinarian show you how to clip nails, and buy a nail clipper to do it yourself. Keep your dog tangle-free, as groomers charge extra for matted dogs.

License: Up to $60 per year. Most urban areas require annual licenses for dogs, although many rural areas do not. The fee for spayed and neutered dogs is often less than that for intact dogs.

Fence or containment: $200–$2000 and up. The best containment system is a fence, but you can also use a kennel run. The fence should be secure enough to keep other dogs out.

Home repair: $15 and up (and up and up). Chewed furniture, shredded carpet, new paint for doors, and replacement screens for windows are the most common projects. Count on carpet cleaning. Keeping your puppy confined in a dog-proof area when you can't watch him will cut down on repair bills.

Note: Costs in metropolitan areas tend to be higher than costs in rural areas.

Leadership

Aussies were bred to boss around livestock. Convincing a recalcitrant steer that it needs to go the other way takes a dog with a pushy personality who doesn't necessarily take no for an answer. Aussies can tend to push your limits, as well. They will test your rules and your commands. Despite being a naturally obedient breed, they also tend to think for themselves, and often consider their choices far superior to yours. At times you'll need to assert yourself and not let your Aussie take over if you are to remain the leader. If you let your Aussie walk all over you, he'll take charge of the household and things will not go well.

While positive training techniques work best for obedience lessons, there are times when a correction will be necessary. Because the breed was created to withstand some tough treatment from livestock, physical corrections may go unnoticed unless accompanied by stern words. Many Aussies are more upset by verbal corrections than physical ones. Corrections need not be harsh, but they do need to be consistent.

Consistency is key when it comes to training, as Aussies tend to take advantage of what they see as loopholes in the rules. An Aussie rewarded for begging "just this once" won't stop there; he's likely to steal the food right off your plate next time. An Aussie allowed to tug you on the leash so he can check out an interesting scent is likely to pull you off your feet so he can chase a cat. You must set up rules early on, and stick to them. Aussies actually do better with a benign dictatorship than they do with a laissez-faire leadership style. This doesn't mean you need to be rough or unloving—just firm, fair, and consistent.

Socialization

Some dogs are happy minding their own business in another part of the house. Not Aussies. They will want to be in the same room with you, to the point that if you get up to go to the bathroom, they'll trot alongside for the big event. And then keep you company!

Although Aussies are all-weather dogs that can adapt to fairly hot weather and fairly cold weather well, they are not really outdoor dogs. They are not temperamentally suited to going without human company. While another dog will fill the void when you're not around, your Aussie will never be satisfied unless he can spend a good part of his day with you, whether you're indoors or out.

Aussies and Kids

An Australian Shepherd can be a child's perfect companion—but it depends on the dog and how you teach both dog and child to interact.

Aussies tend to be extremely tolerant of pokes, tugs, and even being fallen upon. And at least most Aussies can't get their tails pulled! They are

not overreactive to stimuli, and they are not fragile in the event a child does fall on one. Aussies love to snuggle, and don't be surprised if your dog picks your child's bed as his sleeping quarters. Aussies are kids at heart. They love companionship and games. What could be better than having a built-in playmate in the form of a child?

Aussies seem to realize they must be gentle and careful with small children. Nonetheless, because of their size and boisterous nature, it's probably best to hold off adding one to your household until your children are past the toddler stage—or at least swoop the kid out of the way when you're getting ready to take the dog for a walk!

Aussies can be taught not to pull on a leash, so that a child can walk them. However, it's never a good idea to send a child and dog out alone. Dogs can be tempted to take chase, pulling away from the child, or another dog can cause problems.

FYI: Aussie Physical Considerations

Besides behavioral considerations, your choice of an Aussie should involve some consideration of his physical attributes.

Size: Aussies are medium-sized dogs, ranging in height from 18 to 21 inches (about 46 to 53 cm) for females and 20 to 23 inches (about 51 to 58 cm) for males. Females generally weigh from about 35 to 55 pounds (about 16 to 25 kg), and males from 45 to 65 pounds (about 20 to 29 kg). They are compactly built and can fit in relatively small spaces for their size. The fact that most are tailless means that you don't have to worry about a long wagging tail clearing your coffee table!

Grooming: The Aussie coat is low-maintenance. It is not prone to matting, although some more heavily coated dogs can form mats in their long britches or in the silky hair behind their ears. Mud and dirt tend to fall off the coat—usually inside your house, of course. Washing will make the coat softer and fluffier, but it isn't really necessary unless the dog has rolled in something disgusting.

Parasites can be difficult to notice under a thick coat, but flea prevention treatments can usually fend off flea infestations. Ticks may be harder to prevent; in tick areas you will need to run your fingers through your dog's coat every day.

Aussies do shed a good amount. The more often you brush them, the less hair will be shed in your house. But even if you brush a lot, be prepared to buy a powerful vacuum cleaner and to use it every few days.

Health: Aussies are typically healthy, and live well into their teens. Some double merles (see page 27) may have problems with deafness and possibly vision. The major hereditary problems in the breed are cataracts and epilepsy. See page 95 for more details on hereditary predispositions.

Aussies are protective of their families, but can discriminate between real danger and false alarms. This means they will very likely protect a child against a real threat but ignore the screams of your child and her friends playing. Of course, any young child should always be supervised when with a dog, even the most trusted dog.

Aussies and Other People

Aussies are a protective ranch dog, bred to not only herd livestock but also to protect the stock and the homestead against intruders. As such, Aussies don't tend to be the social butterflies that some other herding breeds are. They are one-family dogs that are reserved, even wary, with strangers. This may be confused with shyness but is more often just the breed's natural caution. Should a stranger actually threaten, the typical Aussie will not back down. It takes them a while to accept strangers as friends, and even then, they still tend to save their real trust for their family. This inborn wariness means that Aussie owners must make special efforts to ensure their Aussies are well socialized (see page 44).

Because of their guardian nature, Aussies will act protectively if you are threatened by another person. If the threat seems real, they may even bite. Don't put your Aussie in a situation where he might perceive a person as threatening who isn't, and possibly be blamed for an unprovoked bite. But in most cases, he can tell the difference. An Aussie is not itching to bite anyone, but he's ready if he has no other choice when it comes to protecting his family.

Particularly during a young Aussie's adolescence, wariness and aggressiveness may be accentuated. Aussies may growl at people they don't like and may even charge at them if they seem threatening. You must continue to socialize and train your youngster to accept people during this time. With continued work, the typical Aussie will grow out of this phase and settle down to be a tolerant, if not necessarily gregarious, adult.

Aussies and Other Pets

Australian Shepherds have a strong sense of family, and that usually extends to other dogs and pets in the household. Although some can be pushy to the point of trying to dominate other dogs, most coexist peacefully with others.

As herding dogs, Aussies have a partially developed prey drive. Herding is actually a truncated form of hunting, in which the stalk and chase part of the process is accentuated, and the catch (and kill) part is diminished. Thus, don't be surprised if your Aussie stalks and chases squirrels, cats, and livestock outdoors. But your cats, and cats indoors, are different; they are usually accepted as family members and considered off-limits for chasing. It's not unusual for Aussies and cats to cuddle together and become good friends.

Bad Habits

All dogs have bad habits and behaviors. Some breeds are predisposed to act in ways that are good for the job they were bred to do, but bad for life in a more urban environment.

Barking All dogs bark to some extent. Aussies bark a little bit more than average, but not excessively. Barking is part of what Aussies need to do to fulfill their role of herder and guardian. Unlike breeds that move sheep by crouching and staring, Aussies do so more forcefully, using barking as a means to get them moving away. They also bark to warn the family of intruders and to scare away those intruders.

Barking has been selected by humans during the course of canine domestication, particularly by people who wanted a dog to herd and defend. One popular theory of dog domestication speculates that domestic dogs are neotenized wolves—that is, wolves in various stages of arrested development. Adult wolves almost never bark, but adult dogs do. Like young wolves, adult dogs remain comparatively trustful, playful, dependent, obedient—and barky. In some ways, herding is a behavior of young, not adult, wolves as well, as it emphasizes the stalk and chase part of the hunt, without the kill.

Don't get an Aussie, or any dog, if you demand silence. But just because it's natural doesn't mean you have to let your Aussie bark unchecked. See page 72 for ways of coping with excessive barking.

Digging Digging is a natural and adaptive behavior. Wild dogs dig for a number of reasons. They excavate dens in which to raise young, and they bury food for later consumption. They dig out prey. Young wolves practice digging as part of their play repertoire, and because domestic dogs retain so many behaviors of young wolves, they include digging as part of their day's entertainment. Fortunately, Aussies are not big diggers. As long as your Aussie gets adequate mental and physical stimulation, digging probably won't be considered high-priority entertainment.

Chewing All dogs, especially puppies, like to chew. Puppies explore with their teeth by carrying, licking, grabbing, biting, and gnawing. Even adults enjoy chewing, but usually you can redirect it to more acceptable targets, such as chew toys and rawhides. Aussies are not particularly mouth-oriented dogs, but they will chew if given the chance, especially if they are bored or frustrated because of too little exercise. See page 51 for advice on coping with chewing.

Stealing Dogs evolved as hunters and scavengers. Anything left unguarded was fair game and ended up in a smart dog's mouth. Ranch dogs were taught not to steal eggs or cooling pies, but smart ranchers and ranch wives knew it was far wiser to keep supper out of reach. You can train your Aussie not to steal from countertops, but it's a lot smarter to never keep food where he can get to it. That goes for both your lunch and your garbage pail. Aussies like to eat, and sometimes their stomachs override their conscience—and they're not too discriminating!

Chapter Three

How to Choose an Australian Shepherd

Finding an Australian Shepherd is easy. Check the classifieds, surf the Internet, ask a neighbor—but the more choices you have, the more you'll come to realize that not all Aussies are created equal. Some have the potential to be healthier than others, or better at particular tasks, or just plain prettier. Some come from responsible breeders who've provided the best puppy care and socialization, whereas others come from breeders who either don't know or don't care about such things. You can still get a good Aussie from a bad source, but why buck the odds?

The Best Source

Breeders who are careful about the dogs they breed, the way they are raised, and the homes they go to are more likely to have Aussies with good health, good temperament, and good looks. Such breeders are also more likely to be accessible throughout your Aussie's life to advise you on the latest dilemma, and share in the latest anecdote, celebrate his accomplishments, and even console you after your dog passes away. With such a breeder you may find yourself part of an extended family of puppy owners, and you can keep up with your dog's littermates throughout their lives. Should circumstances arise that force you to surrender your dog, good breeders are there to make sure he is taken care of.

Such breeders often make producing quality Aussies their life's passion. They may breed for show, obedience, or herding competition, or for superior companion or working dogs. They evaluate the puppies with a critical eye, so that even puppies from the best litters may not all make the grade for competition. Such puppies will be sold as companion (or pet) quality for more affordable prices compared to their competition-quality littermates.

Good Aussie breeders love their breed, but they are the first to tell you that Aussies aren't for everyone. They are less interested in making a sale than they are in ensuring the puppy is going to a good home where he will spend his entire life. If a breeder doesn't quiz you about your home, intentions, and activity level, and doesn't warn you about the Aussie's need for something to do, be suspicious.

Good breeders will ask about your experience with dogs, and with herding dogs and Aussies in particular. They will ask about your facilities and family. They will discuss expenses, training, exercise, and safety issues with you. They may require that you neuter or spay your dog. A breeder who doesn't care where her puppies are going probably doesn't care where they came from either, and there's a good chance very little thought went into breeding and raising the litter.

Finding a Good Breeder

The best place to find good breeders is through Australian Shepherd clubs and competitions. Your choice of club may depend upon your intentions with your dog.

If you want to compete in ASCA events, go to *www.asca.org*, click on "Finding an Aussie," and then click on "Breeder Directory." You can also click on "ASCA Information" and then "Affiliate Clubs" to find a local Aussie club that might be able to recommend a local breeder or even a litter. If you'd rather compete in AKC events, start with the United States Australian Shepherd Club at *www.australianshepherds.org*; click on "Finding a Puppy," and then "Breeder Directory." Of course, it never hurts to search both sites. Choosing a breeder from these sites doesn't guarantee that you'll get a better Aussie, but it does make it more likely.

You can find local Aussie clubs by going to the AKC site at *www.akc.org*, and clicking on "Clubs" and then "Club Search." To find Aussie clubs select "Specialty" when prompted for the type of club. You can also search for local all-breed, obedience, and herding clubs. Having a local breeder is a great advantage, because you can get to know the breeder and his or her dogs firsthand, and they also can get to know you. Having your breeder close by is especially helpful for training

advice and for keeping in touch with an extended Aussie family.

A great way to meet breeders and see lots of Aussies is to attend a dog show, especially an Australian Shepherd specialty show. A specialty show is a prestigious event just for one breed. The National Specialty show is the premier event for the breed, attracting hundreds of Aussies competing in conformation, obedience, herding, and other venues. Information about the USASA National can be found at *www.australianshepherds.org*, and details on the ASCA National can be found at *www.asca.org* (click on "Events"). You can find a local all-breed dog show by going to *www.akc.org*, click on "Events" and then "Event and Awards Search."

You can also locate good breeders in Australian Shepherd and all-breed dog magazines, or join one of the many online Aussie discussion lists and get to know breeders there. Try to find a group that has interests in various dog competitions and activities, rather than ones populated by pet owners comparing cute stories—although those are worth joining for fun!

What Age

The best time to bring a new puppy home is between 7 and 12 weeks of age. Before 7 weeks, removing a puppy from his dam and littermates deprives him of learning essential canine social skills. After 12 weeks, puppies naturally become more fearful of new situations. However, especially if the breeder has taken measures to expose the puppy to new experiences and people, an older puppy can also make the transition just fine. Don't hesitate to welcome a well-adjusted Aussie of any age into your home. In fact, an adult Aussie, especially an older one, is a great choice if you value your furniture, rugs, and sanity, and want a calmer dog.

Performance and Competition

If you're contemplating using your Aussie as a stockdog or in competitive activities, your criteria will need to be a little more demanding. Good health should always be a priority, but you also want to get a dog from lines that are already proven in those areas.

Conformation Aussies need to come from ASCA or AKC lines. The pedigree should be replete with Champion (abbreviated "Ch") titles before the dogs' names. If your interest is in herding, obedience, or agility, look for pedigrees featuring dogs with titles in those venues (see pages 126, 127, 131, and 132 for a list of such titles).

Health

Most people who are looking for an Aussie first of all want a good healthy companion, and most Aussies are quite healthy. But like most breeds, Australian Shepherds have some hereditary health problems that are more common in them than in some other breeds. By screening the parents, responsible breeders can choose not to breed dogs with a greater likelihood of passing on such traits. Australian Shepherd health researchers highly recommend screening for hip dysplasia, elbow dysplasia, and eye problems before breeding; they also suggest testing for thyroid problems, Collie eye anomaly, and drug sensitivity.

The Orthopedic Foundation for Animals (OFA) and the Canine Eye Registration Foundation (CERF) screen and register dogs for certain genetic health issues. Dogs that have OFA numbers for hips and elbows, and CERF numbers for eyes, are issued a Canine Health Information Center (CHIC) number and appear in the CHIC database (*www.caninehealthinfo.org*). You can search for particular dogs, or search in general to see if one kennel has a lot of CHIC dogs (indicating an interest in producing healthy Aussies) by clicking on "Search CHIC Breeds" and entering "Australian Shepherds" in the breed choice box. Most breeders use the same kennel name as a prefix, so dogs beginning with the same name are usually from the same breeder.

Hip dysplasia, a common problem of large breeds, is not actually a widespread ailment in Aussies. In fact, according to the OFA, Aussies rank 122nd out of 150 breeds in terms of the incidence of hip dysplasia, with only about 6 percent dysplastic. Only about 4 percent are reported with elbow dysplasia. You can search the OFA database by going to *www.ofa.org*, and clicking on "Search OFA Records." Despite the fact that these conditions are not rampant in the breed, they still can't be ignored, and all breeding stock should be screened.

Epilepsy is the Aussie's most common serious health problem, but no screening tests are available for it. You may be able to ask the breeder for the health records of the parents to show that they do not have the condition.

No knowledgeable or ethical breeder would breed a dog with epilepsy.

Hereditary cataracts are the eye disease of most concern in Aussies. These cataracts occur earlier in life than do those associated with old age, and they may become so bad that the lens needs to be removed. A DNA test is available for the gene that causes the majority (but not all) of the cases of cataracts in Aussies. A dog with just one copy of the mutant gene can develop hereditary cataracts and should not be bred.

Breeders should have the DNA test results for MDR1 drug sensitivity for both parents. If both parents are negative, the puppy will be negative as well and will not need to be tested. Otherwise you will want to test your dog before he receives any drugs that dogs with this mutation are sensitive to. See page 110 for more information.

FYI: Double Danger

You may be captivated by a mostly white Aussie puppy, or interested in a breeding between two merle Aussies. In either case, you're better to walk away. The merle coat pattern is caused by the action of one dominant gene. Most merles you see have one such *M* gene and one recessive *m* gene. When two merles are bred together, on average about a quarter of the puppies will inherit the *M* gene from both parents and thus will have two *M* genes: *MM*. These homozygous merles tend to have unusually large areas of white in their fur, which is why the breed standard disqualifies dogs from competition that have as little as one third of the coat covered in white. Homozygous merles also tend to be deaf, blind, or both to some degree; most dogs have unusually small or even absent eyes. Some reports also attribute cardiac, skeletal, and reproductive problems to homozygous merles. This is why responsible breeders don't breed merles to one another and don't sell predominantly white puppies if such breedings occur. It's possible to accidentally breed two merles together if one or both of them are cryptic (or phantom) merles—that is, they have so little merle patterning that they appear to be non-merles except on close inspection. Controversy exists over whether cryptic merles bred to one another produce the same sort of problems that obvious merle-to-merle matings create. A DNA test was at one time available to detect the merle gene but is no longer on the market.

If Collie eye anomaly (CEA), progressive retinal atrophy (PRA), or cobalamin malabsorption has been reported in either parent's family, that parent at least should have a DNA test for the condition. It's fine to breed carriers—just not to each other.

In general, ask to see a copy of any DNA or screening test results for parents or puppies. For more information on hereditary health concerns, see Chapter 6.

What the Pedigree Tells You

Your Aussie's pedigree is a story of who begat whom that can be traced back until the first Aussies were registered. Because of space constraints, however, most pedigrees only show you the most recent few generations. Read a pedigree from left to right, with your puppy on the left, his sire to the right and above, and his dam to the right and below.

Avoid inbred pedigrees, in which the same dog appears as an ancestor of both your puppy's sire and dam. The fewer generations between that dog and the litter generally means a more inbred litter. Although inbreeding is a tool used by many breeders, it increases the chance of two recessive genes appearing in a puppy, and thus the likelihood of certain health problems.

Picking the Puppy

A litter of Aussies looks like a pile of teddy bears. Not surprisingly, there's something about each one that will steal your heart. But try to steel yourself to make an honest evaluation of them. Aussie puppies sleep hard and play hard, so if they are sleeping, you may have to wait to see them at their best. Aussie puppies should be friendly toward you; avoid puppies that growl or snap at you, or ones that freeze, cringe, or urinate when you pick them up. You want a puppy that enjoys being with his littermates, but enjoys being with you even more.

There's nothing wrong with choosing the puppy that seems to choose you, or with letting the breeder choose the puppy. After all, there's no way you can get to know them in the short time you'll be there like the breeder has gotten to know them.

Puppy Aptitude Tests

Puppy aptitude tests can give you a hint of how the puppies in a litter measure up against each other and puppies from other litters. Optimally, the

PERSONALITY POINTERS
Puppy Aptitude Test

Test/Purpose	How to Test	What to Look For	Results
Social attraction Measures sociability and dependence	The tester coaxes the puppy toward her.	Does the puppy come eagerly, eventually, or not at all?	The faster the puppy comes, the better.
Following Measures dependence versus independence	The tester walks away.	Does the puppy follow eagerly, hesitantly, or not at all?	The more eagerly the puppy follows, the better.
Restraint Measures dominance versus submissiveness	The tester gently rolls the puppy on his back and holds him there.	Does the puppy fight it, eventually relax, or give up immediately?	The more a puppy fights, the greater his tendency to be dominant.
Social dominance Measures dominance versus submissiveness	The tester strokes the standing puppy on the back.	Does the puppy protest, lick the tester, try to escape, or roll over?	An intermediate response is usually best.
Elevation dominance Measures acceptance of dominance when the puppy has no control	The tester lifts the pup slightly off the ground and holds him there.	Does the puppy struggle fiercely, accept it, try to lick, or freeze?	An intermediate response is usually best.
Retrieving	The tester tosses a crumpled-up piece of paper.	Does the pup fetch it, grab it and run away, or just look?	A pup that runs after it and brings it back is a better dog for retrieving.
Sound sensitivity	The tester makes a sharp noise a few feet from the puppy.	Does the puppy bark at it, look at it, or cringe?	Barking or looking are good responses.
Touch sensitivity	The tester presses the webbing between the toes.	How long does it take the puppy to protest?	A medium sensitivity is probably best.
Sight sensitivity	The tester jerks a towel on a string near the puppy.	Does the puppy give chase, just look, or run away?	A puppy that looks is probably best.

tests are given as close to when the puppy is 49 days old as possible, and the tester should be a stranger to the puppy. If your heart is set on a puppy but the test says otherwise, come back and try him again. The tests are far from infallible and, in fact, probably don't have that much predictive value for adult behavior. But they can evaluate the puppy at the time in his life you take him home. And they're fun! The test consists of nine parts.

Puppy Health

The breeder should have wormed the puppy and given him one or two sets of vaccinations, depending on age. The puppy should also have been examined by a veterinarian, and the veterinary records, including vaccination history, should be available. However, any sale should be contingent upon a veterinary examination at your expense within 48 hours. Your veterinarian is in the best position to evaluate the puppy's health. Before choosing your puppy, you can do your own preliminary health check.

- The skin should not have parasites, hair loss, crusts, or reddened areas.
- The eyes, ears, and nose should be free of discharge.
- None of the puppies should be coughing, sneezing, or vomiting.
- The area around the anus should have no hint of irritation or recent diarrhea.
- Puppies should be neither thin nor potbellied.
- The gums should be pink, not pale.
- The eyelids and lashes should not fold in on the eyes.
- By the age of 12 weeks, males should have both testicles descended into the scrotum.
- Avoid any puppy that is making significant breathing sounds, including excessive wheezing or snorting.

Paperwork

Your purebred Australian Shepherd should come with the following paperwork:

- Registration slip
- Bill of sale
- Copy of the pedigree
- Record of the puppy's medical information
- Any contract or health guarantee
- Contact information in case of future questions
- Care instructions

Fun Facts

What's in a Name?

Often hobby breeders will require that their kennel name be part of the dog's registered name, usually the first name. Some breeders also use litter identifiers, requesting that you name your puppy starting with a certain letter or theme. That way other breeders know that all the puppies whose names start with the letter "D" or with the name of some songbird, for example, are littermates. The NSDR only allows short names made up of your last name (or a kennel name if it is registered with them) and the dog's call name.

Rescue

Good breeders make every attempt to place their Aussies in homes where they will be loved forever. If the homes don't work out, they are ready to take the dogs back. But not all Aussies come from such breeders, and even those that do sometimes find themselves homeless.

Rescue Aussies come in all ages, from all circumstances, and in all conditions. Most often it's just a case of the wrong home for the dog. People who thought they understood the meaning of "active dog" found out they didn't. They got fed up with behavior problems that they caused themselves by not properly exercising or training their dogs. Some people who promised to provide a home for life found their situation changed to the point they couldn't fulfill their promise. Some Aussies simply become lost. Sometimes owners die without having made provisions for their dogs.

Helpful Hints

Rescue Resources

Aussie Rescue and Placement Helpline: *www.aussierescue.org*

Second Time Around Aussie Rescue: *www.staar.org*

PetFinder: *www.petfinder.org* (national database of all breeds in shelters)

You can also contact local breed clubs or search the Internet for "Australian Shepherd Rescue" for local Aussie rescue groups.

Rescue dogs have already had their hearts broken, and they need secure, permanent homes where it won't happen again. That's one reason rescue groups are picky about where these dogs go. Most begin the adoption process by having prospective owners complete an application. Applicants may be asked to provide veterinary references, and the rescue group may schedule a phone interview or home visit. Although this may seem invasive, it's partly to make the best match of dog and family.

Many rescue groups provide temperament testing, basic training, and behavior consultation. Adopting from a rescue group provides new owners with a safety net should problems arise. Many groups require adoptive owners to enroll in obedience classes in order to encourage bonding, basic dog training skills, and basic manners. They also often provide opportunities to become a club member, participate in Aussie activities and rescue reunions, and even become part of the rescue team.

Some people think that rescue dogs are free. They aren't. Not only do people tend to value objects or pets they have an investment in more than those they don't, but rescue groups need to charge a reasonable fee in order to recoup their expenses and continue to provide services.

Some rescues are less expensive than others, however. Generally, an Aussie from a county shelter is the least expensive, while those from Aussie rescue groups cost more. Dogs from the latter are usually examined for health and temperament problems, and treated as needed, so the costs tend to even out. Regardless, a rescue dog is the deal of a lifetime.

10 **Questions** to Ask the Breeder ▰▰▰▰▰▰

1 **Do you specialize in Australian Shepherds?**

Good breeders work with only one or two breeds of dogs, so they can concentrate on just those breeds. Breeders with a smorgasbord of breeds and crossbreeds tend to be in the business of producing puppies for profit and may not be as selective in choosing parents.

2 **Do you have litters available all the time?**

Good breeders seldom have puppies available without putting you on a waiting list. That's because they don't breed a lot, and their dogs are in demand. They may have dogs they have chosen not to breed because, in the breeder's opinion, they may not produce good puppies. In contrast, poor breeders consider the fact that a dog has registration papers to be quality enough, even if he has poor temperament or health.

3 **Can I visit or see a video of the dam and the puppies in their environment?**

Good breeders are proud of their dogs and facilities. It used to be that a home visit was a necessity, but because of safety issues, more breeders are wary about inviting relative strangers into their homes. But you should be able to see pictures or a video of the puppies in their environment.

4 **How did you choose these parents?**

Good breeders should be able to discuss the merits and possible shortcomings of both parents, and why they chose to breed them.

5 **Can I see the pedigree?**

Good breeders have the pedigree on hand, without searching or sending for it. In fact, good breeders will also have pictures and knowledge of many of the dogs in the pedigree for several generations back.

6 **Are the puppies registered?**

Good breeders will have AKC, ASCA, or NSDR registered dogs (or their dogs will be registered with the national kennel club in whatever country they're in). The United Kennel Club is the only other acceptable registry in the United States.

7 **Is there a written sales agreement?**

Good breeders will supply a written agreement that includes the registration information, price, and any conditions.

8 **What sort of health screening have the parents had?**

Good breeders will have OFA numbers for hip and elbow dysplasia clearances, and CERF numbers or copies of screening results for eye clearances. They should have DNA test results for cataracts and MDR1 for both parents. They should offer a health warranty that guarantees the puppy's health, barring accident, for about a week after you've taken possession and under certain conditions. They will not, however, guarantee the puppy's health for years, because nobody can make such a promise. As with all living beings, dogs can become prematurely ill, or suffer from unforeseen hereditary problems.

9 What health tests have the puppies had?

The breeder should have the puppies' eyes examined by a veterinary ophthalmologist when they are between 5 and 8 weeks of age, as this is when signs of Collie eye anomaly can most easily be identified. The exam should also check for iris coloboma, distichiasis, and persistent pupillary membrane. In addition, the puppies should have their hearts checked by a veterinarian before being placed. They should have had one set of puppy vaccinations and any necessary worming.

10 What do you need from me?

Good breeders ask for more than money. In fact, that's the last thing they mention. They want evidence that you're going to be a good home for their puppy for life. If they don't care where their puppies are going, they probably don't care much about them in general.

Chapter Four

Caring for an Australian Shepherd Puppy

T he first year with your new Aussie will be a lot of work, but even more fun. The foundations you lay now can be the difference between a good relationship and a bad one, and even life and death. So take the trouble to do it right—and have fun! But even before your puppy arrives home there are rooms to puppy-proof, things to buy, and classes to investigate.

Aussie Accessorizing

Aussies aren't particularly materialistic dogs. Give them a place to play and a person to play with, and they're pretty much happy. But of course you'll need more than that—and half the fun of a new dog is going on a shopping spree.

Consider the following items:

Crate Crates come in three types: wire, which fold flat and have better ventilation; plastic, which are cozy and approved for airline shipping; and cloth, which are lightweight but can be shredded by dogs who want out. Cloth crates are not recommended unless you can be there supervising, and even then, you may have to be quick to prevent a rip!

Exercise pen An exercise pen (X-pen) is a doggy playpen that you can set up inside. It's safer than locking your puppy in a bathroom, and he's less likely to object because it doesn't have that closed-in feeling that a small room gives him. Choose one that's about 3 to 4 feet (1 m) high. Set the pen in your kitchen or den, where he can be out from underfoot yet still part of the family when you can't watch him. You can also take the X-pen on trips so that you have a portable yard; this is especially handy at rest stops or campgrounds. *Optional.*

Baby gates Baby gates allow your dog more freedom while blocking off restricted areas. Don't use the old-fashioned accordion style, which can close on a puppy's neck. If you don't care about home fashion, just prop a long, sturdy piece of cardboard in your doorway.

Fence If you have a yard and plan to let your dog loose in it, you need a fence. The Aussie is a problem solver, so make sure the fence is Aussie-proof from the start. The fence needs to be at least 4 feet (approx. 2 m) tall. Ideally, a fenced area extends from the back door so that you can just open the door to let him out.

Kennel If you plan to leave your Aussie outside while you can't supervise, consider a kennel run. A run with a cover is especially helpful for jumpers and climbers.

Bed Aussies consider themselves tough dogs, but even they appreciate a soft bed. A cushion or blanket will do fine.

Anti-chew spray Like an off-limits sign for your furniture legs, these sprays taste so bitter your puppy will practically foam at the mouth if he tries to chew on something that you've sprayed. *Optional.*

Collar or harness Not just a fashion statement, a collar or harness is a means of controlling and identifying your dog. Make sure a collar is loose enough for you to get a couple of fingers between it and your puppy's neck, but not so loose that it could slide over his head when walking on leash. Don't leave a puppy with a collar unattended, because pups have a talent for getting their lower jaw stuck in them.

Leash Start with a sturdy lightweight leash, 4 to 6 feet (about 1 to 2 m) long. Don't get a chain leash, which will hurt your hands if the dog tugs.

Retractable leash Retractable leashes give your dogs more freedom, but too many people give them so much freedom that the dog wanders into the road, or up to strange dogs or under people's feet. Retractable leashes should be retracted unless you're in a safe place away from other people and dogs. *Optional.*

Identification Almost any large pet supply store sells identification tags you can make on the spot. Get one.

Cleaning supplies For rug accidents, use an enzymatic carpet cleaner, which destroys the odor-causing molecules rather than simply covering them up.

Poop scoop If you have a yard, don't try to clean it with makeshift trowels and buckets; use a tool designed to make the job easy. Two-part scoops are easier to use than hinged versions. Scoops with a rake on one side are better for grass, and the flat-edge pusher varieties are better for cement surfaces.

Poop bags A variety of special doggy poop disposal bags are available, but you can also use a baby diaper disposal bag or a cheap sandwich bag.

Bowls You can use your own bowls or buy dog bowls. Stainless bowls are easy to clean and durable. Ceramic bowls have the disadvantage of chipping. Plastic bowls are the least preferred, because the scratches hold germs, and some dogs are allergic to them.

Self-feeding and self-watering bowls These bowls refill when depleted. Just make sure to check that they're still full every day. The disadvantage is that they make it hard to monitor your dog's eating and drinking, and food and water can become old and stagnant. You still have to wash the bowl regularly. *Optional.*

Brush A soft-bristle brush is ideal for getting your puppy used to grooming. Later, you can buy more appropriate grooming tools for his longer coat.

Rinseless shampoo When you can't give your dog a real bath, just squirt some rinseless shampoo on him, rub it in, and wipe the dirt away with a towel. *Optional.*

Grooming table A table with a grooming arm can save your back and keep your dog under control. *Optional.*

Toothbrush For now, you just need a soft baby toothbrush and some doggy toothpaste, so that your puppy can get used to the feel of having his teeth brushed.

Toenail clippers Start clipping the tips of your puppy's nails now so that he gets used to it.

Plush toys Puppies love soft fuzzy toys. Make sure no parts can come off, and that your puppy can't gut the toy and swallow any noisemakers. Avoid bean or Styrofoam stuffing. Warning: Many Aussies immediately dissect plush toys, ripping the stuffing from them.

Throw toys Balls and other toys, such as tug toys, that encourage playing with people are especially good for social development. Studies have shown that dogs that don't get a chance to retrieve as puppies are far less likely to do so as adults.

Interactive toys Toys that challenge your puppy to dislodge food treats can occupy him while you're away. Rotate several interactive toys with different challenges to prevent him from getting bored.

CHECKLIST

Puppy-Proofing

Check all over your house for:

- ✔ uncovered electrical outlets (can cause shocks)
- ✔ open stairways, decks, or balconies (can cause falls)
- ✔ unsecured doors (can allow escapes, or slam shut on puppy)

Check the kitchen for:

- ✔ open cabinets holding cleaners and degreasers (can invite poisoning)
- ✔ accessible garbage with enticing rancid food and splintering bones (can invite poisoning, sickness, or gut injury)
- ✔ plastic wraps that can be swallowed (can lodge in intestines)

Check the dining room for:

- ✔ hanging table cloths that, if pulled, can bring dishes crashing down (can crush or otherwise injure puppy)
- ✔ swinging doors (can trap puppy's head and neck)

Check the family room for:

- ✔ fireplace without a secure fire screen (can burn puppy)
- ✔ craft or sewing kits (needles and thread can be swallowed, causing severe injury and illness)
- ✔ heavy statues or vases (can fall on puppy)

Check the bedrooms for:

- ✔ children's toys (can chew off pieces)
- ✔ open closets, especially shoe closets (can chew up your shoes)

Check the bathrooms for:

- ✔ pills and medicines (only takes a few to poison a puppy)
- ✔ hair treatments (can cause eye injuries)
- ✔ drain cleaners (can poison)
- ✔ razors (can be swallowed)
- ✔ diaper pails (disposable diapers can be eaten and swell in stomach)

Check the garage for:

- ✔ antifreeze (one swallow can cause fatal kidney failure)
- ✔ fuels, cleaners, and paints (can be toxic)
- ✔ batteries (battery acid can be toxic)
- ✔ nails and screws (can cause gut injuries)
- ✔ herbicides, insecticides, and fertilizers (can be toxic)
- ✔ rodent bait (can be enticing to eat, but fatal)

Check the yard for:

- ✔ weak fence (puppy can escape and/or be harmed)
- ✔ rotten tree limbs (can fall on puppy)
- ✔ unfenced pool (can drown puppy; always have a way for a dog to climb out, and teach him to find and use it)
- ✔ cocoa mulch (contains theobromine, which is poisonous to dogs)
- ✔ fruit and nut trees (some nuts and fruit parts are poisonous)
- ✔ pointed sticks at eye level (can poke into running puppy's eye)
- ✔ predators (can carry off a small dog)
- ✔ treated lawns (can contain toxic chemicals that puppy may lick off his paws)
- ✔ poisonous plants (can be eaten)
- ✔ insect hives (digging or playing puppy can cause insects to attack)

First Impressions

It's natural to want to share the excitement of welcoming home your new dog with friends and neighbors. But it's not fair to your dog, who will already be confused enough. Make it easy for him to figure out who the important people in his new life will be. Introduce him only to family for now; there will be plenty of time for him to play socialite later.

If it's a fairly short drive from the breeder's, arrange to pick up the puppy before the breeder has fed him his next scheduled meal, so he'll be hungry when he arrives at your house. This way you can immediately feed him, giving him a chance to identify you as his new provider. Don't make him go hungry to accomplish this, however; most Aussies will eat eagerly no matter how recently they've been fed!

Before you go inside your house, give the puppy a chance to relieve himself in the area you've decided will be his outdoor bathroom area. It's never too soon to start good habits. Then let him explore in the yard or house—always supervised, of course. Once inside, feed him in a secure place such as his crate or X-pen. Then take him outside to eliminate again. Spend some more time with him, and when he starts to tire, put him in his sleeping quarters.

His first night away from his old family is going to be confusing and, very likely, frightening. Don't make him sleep all by himself in another room. Even if you don't intend for him to stay in your bedroom in the future, make an exception so he has some company at first. Besides, you know you really want him sleeping there!

A crate placed by your bed is the ideal place for him to sleep. The crate should have plenty of soft bedding in it, as well as a stuffed toy he can use as a surrogate littermate. If your puppy is too uneasy to fall asleep all alone, let him fall asleep next to you outside the crate. When he's snoozing soundly, pick him up and place him in the crate. He may awaken momentarily but will fall back asleep. Chances are he will wake up crying several times the first few nights. Traditional dog-rearing advice warned owners not to give in to the dog's crying. But ignoring him when he most needs reassurance only teaches him that he can't depend on you for help. Some dog behaviorists now believe such a situation may actually contribute to separation anxiety in adulthood. They instead recommend comforting the puppy if he cries so he learns he has some control over his environment. That doesn't mean you spend the rest of your life rushing in at the slightest cry, but it does mean you acknowledge his distress and attend to his basic needs, such as comforting him or taking him to relieve himself. Then you put him back in his bed.

CAUTION

Crate Safety

The crate is one of the safest spots your puppy can be, but you must do your part. Do not leave a collar on your puppy while he's in the crate. Collars, especially choke collars or collars with tags, can get caught in crate wires. Soft bedding is wonderful for most puppies, but those that chew and swallow it may have to be relegated to surfaces less likely to cause intestinal blockages. If your puppy tends to chew on the wire, he could get his jaw or tooth caught. Discourage such behavior by spraying the wire with anti-chew preparations and by making sure your pup has no issues with being crated.

Crate Training

Crates give your dog a secure bed of his own and give you a place to put him where you won't worry about him. Crates help in housetraining, provide a safe means of car travel, and serve as a safe haven when staying with friends or at hotels. A crate-trained dog will fare better if he has to be crated at the veterinary hospital. That doesn't mean your dog should spend hours and hours crated. Think of a crate as your child's crib. It's a safe place to sleep, but not a place to grow up. And it's certainly not a place for punishment.

Establish a good association with the crate by feeding your dog in it. If he's uneasy about it, just place the food slightly inside the crate at first so he doesn't even have to go inside to eat. Then move it further inside. Finally close the door while he eats, opening it as soon as he finishes. You can probably do this within the period of a day. Soon he will be running to the crate as soon as he sees you with food. If you want, you can now introduce a cue—such as *"Bedtime!"*—for him to go in the crate.

Next extend his time in the crate by giving him chew toys or interactive toys to occupy him, or by making sure he is tired and ready to sleep when you put him inside. Extend his time gradually, always trying to let him out before he has a chance to get bored or vocal. If he does begin to protest, wait until he is momentarily quiet before letting him out. Continue to extend the time he must be quiet before he gets released. Ideally, this would take a week or more. Unfortunately, most people don't have a week to crate train their dog, so the best compromise is to place him in the crate for slightly longer periods many times a day.

Although crates keep your puppy out of trouble, you can't keep him crated all the time. One solution is to set up one or more X-pens or even baby playpens in your favorite rooms. You can interact with your puppy as you go about your business, letting him out when you won't be distracted. You can even tether your puppy to your side by attaching a leash from him to your belt. This way he gets used to paying attention to you and following you, and can't wander off without you noticing. Just be sure you give him warning when you race for the phone!

Housetraining

The best time to start teaching a puppy where to eliminate is between 7 and 9 weeks of age. Before that time, puppies do not seem to learn the concept or control themselves sufficiently. After 9 weeks of age, they seem to prefer using whatever surface or place they were using between 7 and 9 weeks. So it is very important that you make sure your pup has as few chances to go in the wrong places—and as many chances to go in the right places—as possible during this crucial time.

This is one reason that dogs raised in indoor X-pens or kennels may be more difficult to housetrain. If they've been raised indoors beyond 9 weeks of age, they may not recognize grass or the great outdoors as a bathroom area, and may be slow to accept it as such.

It doesn't help that the typical dog owner pushes the puppy out the door and leaves him all alone outside, where the puppy protests, cries, and does just about everything but relieve himself. Once let back inside, though, he relaxes enough to wet all over the floor. No matter how busy you are, early housetraining must be a team sport. Go outside with him! And just as you would train any other behavior, lavish him with praise and, more important, treats for eliminating in the right place. Keep a jar of treats by the door and grab a handful when you go outside with him. Wait until he's just finishing, then heap on the praise and give him a treat. Don't wait until you're back inside; that's too late.

A regular schedule is important for housetraining. You can help your puppy to have regular bowel movements by feeding him on schedule and making sure you don't give him novel foods that may cause diarrhea. You should also take him outside when he awakens, after he eats, and before he goes to bed. You will also need to take him out in between those times. A standard rule of thumb is that a puppy can hold himself for as many hours as he is months old. He can go longer, for instance, overnight, if you don't let him eat or guzzle down water before bed. That in turn means not encouraging vigorous play, which will make him thirsty, before bedtime. And of course, there are limits. Beyond the age of 8 months, the rule comes to a standstill; no dog should be asked to hold it beyond eight hours.

Young puppies avoid eliminating in their sleeping and eating areas, so if you restrict your puppy to a small area he's less likely to eliminate there and will make an effort to hold himself until you let him out. You can use the crate as his small area, making sure it's not so large that he can simply use half of it for his bathroom. If the crate is too large, block off part of it with a box or divider. Confine your puppy when you can't supervise him, but let him out regularly; if you force him to have accidents in the crate, he'll give up trying to hold it at all. When you let him out, take him immediately to his elimination area. Once he's relieved himself, socialize, play, snuggle, and do all the fun things that make having a puppy worth all the work.

Once he's housetrained using the crate, expand his den by placing his bed or crate in a tiny enclosed area only a few feet beyond the boundary of

BE PREPARED! Potty Accidents

Accidents will happen. Your reaction will determine if they happen more or less. Rubbing your dog's nose in a mess, no matter how recently it was deposited, doesn't do anything but make him less kissable and convince him you're strange. Such overzealous corrections, including yelling and spanking, when a puppy goes in the wrong place can work against your housetraining efforts in several ways. First, your dog seldom knows why you're on a rant, and it causes him to distrust you. Second, your unpredictable nature causes him to be nervous, which in turn increases the likelihood he will have to urinate or defecate. Third, if he figures out that it's his pottying that gets you upset, he will avoid doing it anywhere you can see him, including outdoors. Instead, he'll wait until he can sneak into another room where he can do it safely.

That doesn't mean you should just ignore your dog if you catch him in the act. Give a startling "No!" or "Aght!" and scoop him up to scuttle him outside as quickly as possible. Once outside, be sure to reward him when he goes in the right place.

To clean urine, sop up as much as you can with towels or, better, a wet-vac before adding any more moisture. Adding water just takes the urine farther into the carpet pad. If you do add water, you must suction up as much as possible with a carpet cleaner or wet-vac. Add an enzymatic cleaner, and use enough to reach the carpet pad. Let it air dry so the enzymes have time to work on negating the odor.

To clean diarrhea, a wet-vac works wonders. Add water to the waste part of the wet-vac. Then suck up the diarrhea. After most of it is gone, spray the area with water as you suction it up. Finally, add an enzymatic cleaner and leave it. Clean the wet-vac by suctioning up clean water and rinsing the waste part.

his bed. Do everything you can to prevent him from soiling this area; that is, keep him on a frequent outdoor bathroom break schedule. Gradually expand his area as he goes without soiling it, until eventually he has access to an entire room, and then another room . . .

If you can't be home to take him out as often as he needs to go, use puppy urine pads (ask for puppy pee pads in the pet store) or sod sections as an indoor potty area. These can be moved outdoors once soiled to teach your puppy to go there. Newspapers are alright in a pinch, but they aren't absorbent.

Being Alone

Being alone is very stressful to puppies, and even many adult dogs. Your puppy instinctively becomes anxious if he finds himself separated from his caregiver. A puppy that finds himself all alone will cry, howl, and yip,

bringing his mother on the run. If nobody shows up, he will keep crying until he is too exhausted to continue. Naïve owners may think he has gotten over his angst, but exhaustion is not the same as being okay.

Contrary to popular opinion, crates don't seem to make young pups feel more secure. In fact, crated pups (especially those not already familiar with the crate) tend to cry even more than uncrated pups when separated. That's why it may be better to leave your pup in an exercise pen or small, safe room when you first start teaching him to be home alone. You can leave a crate with an open door accessible to him in case he does prefer it.

Giving your puppy something to occupy and comfort him while you are gone is useful, but it depends on what you give. Studies have shown that mirrors and soft cuddly toys are most effective at calming separated puppies, but food has little value—probably because distressed puppies are not hungry puppies. Puppies are comforted by soft, warm, dog-shaped toys; some toys even have a heartbeat, simulating the pup's littermates or dam.

Socializing Your Puppy

What makes some dogs eager to meet new people, have new experiences, and learn new things while others seem to hang back, become frightened, and even bite or run away? In part, these differences are influenced by genes. The only thing you can do to influence them is to choose your puppy from an outgoing family. But these differences are also influenced by experiences, especially early experiences. The process of exposing a puppy to the experiences he'll encounter later in life is called socialization.

Socialization begins within the litter. Dogs that are separated from their dam and littermates too early—before 7 weeks of age—have a hard time interpreting dog language and interacting properly with other dogs. Canine behaviorists believe the best time for puppies to go to their new homes is at 7 to 8 weeks of age, after they've learned about being dogs but before they begin to become fearful of novel situations.

Puppies start off life relatively fearless, but at about 5 weeks of age, they gradually become more cautious of new situations and people. Sometime after 12 weeks of age the fear response becomes the dominant one, making it difficult for the puppy to accept new situations he has never before experienced. This means that you have a deadline to meet, a deadline before which you need to make sure your puppy has experienced a wide range of people, places, and things to prepare him for the rest of his life. This is the process of socialization.

But how do you get your puppy out and about when he hasn't finished his series of puppy vaccinations? There are lots of new experiences that don't involve being around potentially unvaccinated dogs. Going for car rides, hanging out at the post office entrance, shopping at stores that allow but don't attract dogs (some hardware and office supply stores allow dogs), playing at a kids playground (be sure your puppy doesn't leave any mess), and visiting dogless neighbors are all safe methods of accomplishing some, but not all, socialization. No matter what, don't take chances by exposing your puppy to stray dogs or places where strays frequent, or to any place unvaccinated or ill dogs might have been (some disease-causing organisms can survive in the soil and on other surfaces for months). The dog park will have to wait.

Think of socialization as puppy shots for the mind. If your puppy has lots of good experiences with children, and one day a child accidentally falls on him, chances are he will continue to like children. But if the child who fell on him was the first child he ever met, he might conclude that children are dangerous and develop a fear of them. Good experiences are like inoculations against future bad experiences. This is why it's so vital for your puppy to have as many guaranteed good experiences as possible before taking chances on having bad ones. The more you can control your dog's first encounters and outings, the better your chance of preventing him from forming bad associations before he's had a chance to form good ones.

When it comes to socialization, it's the quality, not quantity, that counts. Good intentions can too often lead to bad results if you overwhelm your pup. As with all things puppy, you need to introduce new experiences gradually, never pushing your puppy past the point that he's scared. Fear is easy to learn but hard to unlearn. Your aim is to make your puppy comfortable around strange people, dogs, animals, places, and situations. Introduce him to different floorings, stairs, car rides, and things he'll be doing later in life.

Remember, you want introductions to go well, so it's a good idea if you have control over how meetings go. Ask friends to come over and to greet the puppy as strangers should, which means kneeling down and rubbing him under the chin or on the chest. You'll want your puppy to meet men, women, people in wheelchairs, people with canes, and people of all races, ages, and sizes. He should walk up and down stairs, across all sorts of surfaces, and hear a variety of sounds.

Don't take your puppy into a crowd with the idea of letting him meet lots of people at once. He could be stepped on, or people could start trying to pet him all at once, and he could end up being terrified. It's better for your puppy to meet a few well-chosen people under good circumstances than a horde of humans under overwhelming circumstances.

Don't stop socializing just because your puppy has reached the 12-week milestone. He needs refresher exposures over the next months as well in order to be all that he can be.

Playing with Your Aussie Puppy

Besides being fun for both you and your dog, play has an important role in preparing your puppy for life as an adult. Play helps him develop social and physical skills that he'll need for the rest of his life.

Puppies start to play with their dam and littermates at between 2 and 4 weeks of age. Play with littermates is very important for learning social skills. Puppies enjoy play fighting, and often bite one another (or their dam)

ACTIVITIES Fetch!

The best time to teach your puppy to fetch is as soon as possible. The longer you wait, the greater the chance your Aussie will simply look at you quizzically when you throw something, as if to ask why you don't go get it yourself. Fortunately, most Aussies are enthusiastic retrievers, so you don't have to work at it as hard as owners of many other breeds.

The best place to teach your puppy to fetch is in a hallway. Otherwise you can use a long, lightweight line to prevent the dog from running off with the prize. You want him to learn that he gets rewarded for bringing it back to you. Don't steal the prize from him; trade it for a treat and then give it back or throw it again.

Try tossing the toy so it scoots along the floor, or if you have a small ball, bounce it against the wall. Different dogs are excited by different types of toys and movements. Use a special toy the puppy doesn't get to play with otherwise. Always stop when he still wants to play more.

Once he's got the chase and grab part down, work on having him bring it back. If he knows how to come when called, you can call him, but he may drop the toy first. Or you can run away from him, which will usually have him running to you. If he won't bring it, try giving him less room until he has no choice but to bring it to you, then rewarding him and throwing it again. If you position yourself in the middle of a long hallway, you can take one toy from him and immediately throw another to the opposite end of the hall, a game many puppies relish.

A dog that enjoys fetching is a dog that will enjoy playing with you for years to come. He can even be taught to pick up small things from the ground for you. Don't put off teaching him to fetch!

too hard. When this happens the recipient squeals and, if the biter doesn't stop, refuses to play. This teaches the puppy important communication and bite inhibition skills, and it is one reason puppies should not be separated from their litters before 7 weeks of age. If a puppy is separated earlier, try to find a young playmate for him, or assume the role yourself. If the puppy bites too hard, yell "*Ouch!*" and refuse to play if he continues.

Puppies begin to play with objects between 4 and 5 weeks. It's important to introduce balls, toys, and other safe objects to puppies during this period, as puppies learn specific play habits at an early age. By 8 to 12 weeks of age, you should introduce your puppy to the concept of fetch. Puppies not exposed to fetch at that early age have difficulty understanding it later and may never learn the concept.

Between 2 and 6 months of age, puppy games still center around play fighting. If your puppy has other dogs to play with, that's fine, but you also want him to play with you. When he's playing with people, you need to redirect his play fighting games to something more cooperative, such as fetch. Tug games, while controversial with some trainers who believe they

teach the dog he can beat his owner, are actually fine for most dogs. They can help build confidence in some dogs and are a good source of exercise. Just make sure you both take turns winning!

As your puppy grows, introduce puzzle and interactive toys that require him to work to get treats or smaller toys out of them. Such toys are great for occupying his mind when you can't be with him. Rotate your dog's toys, changing them out every few days, to keep him excited about them.

Between 7 and 12 months of age, much of your puppy's play centers on showing you how much faster, stronger, and smarter he is than you. Competitive games can increase a dog's confidence and readiness to stand up to a human competitor; in most dogs these do not develop into problems, but in some predisposed dogs they don't help matters. Owners can prevent some problems by controlling the situation—that is, by teaching the dog to stop tugging or running on command. Once the dog gives up the toy or stops the behavior, the toy can be thrown and the game continued. Tag games, while tempting, can teach bad habits unless you have a "game over" word that means it's time to quit playing and that he now must come when called. Play is important between owner and dog, but the person should be the one to call the shots.

Games tire your dog mentally and physically, both of which are important for keeping him calm and well behaved at home. Lack of exercise is implicated in many behavioral problems. Play is also important for physical and intellectual development. Puppies run, twist, and wrestle, developing muscles, agility, and strength. By playing games that require your puppy to seek out hidden items, follow scent trails, or make choices, your puppy learns to use his brain and senses. Games can also build confidence in shy dogs, and playing in new situations can help dogs adjust to their environment. Play can be used as a reward for good behavior and is often a better motivator than food for active dogs.

Finally, play is important for bonding between you and your dog. Dogs that play games with people as puppies are more likely to continue to play the same types of games as adults. They interact more with the people they play with. Such dogs are more fun to have around and tend to be more sociable for other people as well.

Puppy Behavior Problems

Very young Aussie puppies are so cute, it's hard to imagine that they will ever do anything but try to please you. In fact, many new Aussie owners are lulled into a sense of false security, thinking their puppies must have been born angels. But wait a few months, and that impression will likely change as puppies test boundaries and get into mischief.

It's difficult not to laugh at some of the bad things puppies do, but try to laugh when your puppy doesn't notice. It's too easy to create behavioral problems by inadvertently reinforcing or encouraging the wrong behaviors. Behaviors that may be cute in a puppy may not be so cute in an adult. Play that involves biting or chasing may or may not create ongoing problems with adult play biting, playing keep-away with stolen household objects, or playing catch-me when called.

Common puppy behavior problems include lack of housetraining, hyperactivity, nipping, chewing, and eating feces.

Lack of housetraining usually stems from giving the puppy too much freedom too quickly. You need to go back to basics and restrict the puppy's access to parts of the house when you can't be with him. Many puppies urinate when they greet their owners; this is called submissive urination and is not a lack of housetraining but a lack of confidence. Most puppies grow out of it, but meanwhile, try not to intimidate or excite the puppy—or at least make sure you're outside when you do!

Helpful Hints

Carsickness

Carsickness is common in puppies. If your puppy experiences carsickness, he will drool, vomit, and have diarrhea. Practice going for extremely short trips to fun places where he can get outside before he gets sick. Drive at a steady speed—acceleration and deceleration, as well as turns, bring on nausea. And keep him up near the front of the car, where there's less swaying. Many people find that feeding the puppy a gingersnap cookie before the trip helps. Your veterinarian can prescribe effective medication in difficult cases.

Hyperactivity is usually just part of being an Aussie puppy. Aussies are energetic, and puppies are extra energetic. Be sure to let your puppy run off his energy a few times a day, but never force him to exercise in the belief that it will tire him out even longer. This can actually be bad for his developing joints. Besides playing active games involving running and tugging, a good way to tire out a puppy is to teach him some obedience exercises or tricks, or take him to obedience class, before naptime.

Nipping is a common complaint with puppies. Puppies naturally play by nipping, and without canine playmates, your pup will turn to you. Some dogs have a greater tendency to nip and mouth than others. Aussies, bred to drive stock by nipping if needed, may sometimes chase and nip at running people in play. When your puppy bites you in play, there's no need to react violently. In fact, grabbing at the puppy may only convince him that you, too, are playing roughly. Chances are he will respond by playing back even more roughly. Puppies react this way to one another, escalating their play-fighting until the going gets so rough one cries uncle and leaves. If a puppy bites another pup too hard, the victim will yelp and quit playing or, some-times, yelp and retaliate. This is a valuable lesson that teaches the pup that if he bites too hard, it's game over.

You can do the same. When your pup chomps down on you, yelp sharply and withdraw from him, standing still and ignoring him for 20 seconds or so. If he stops nipping and behaves, quit your statue act and give him a treat. Remember, it's better to reward proper behavior than to try to quash any bad behavior. Don't just stop him from nipping. Reward him for not nipping by giving him a toy to carry, a ball to chase, or a chewie to gnaw. It's important not to reward the pup for biting. It's fun to wriggle your fingers in front of the puppy's face, pulling them out of reach as he lunges for them. It's fun to run and squeal, and to roughhouse on the floor. But if you want him to stop nipping, you can't do that. You must also convince the rest of your family and any visitors that they must not encourage the puppy to nip.

Eating feces is surprisingly common in puppies. The best prevention is to immediately clean up any feces. If you catch him in the act, give him a stern *"No!"* and a gentle tap on the butt to show him it's not acceptable behavior. You can also sprinkle the feces with red pepper to make it too hot to handle, but some puppies will gulp it down anyway. Your veterinarian can prescribe a food additive that supposedly makes the feces taste bad—or at least worse!

Chewing

All puppies chew when they are teething. But they also chew for fun. Just when you think you're safe, they seem to go through a super chewing stage as they approach their first birthday. The best prevention is vigilance and good housekeeping. Remove everything chewable from your puppy's reach. Puppies especially like to chew stuffed furniture, wooden objects, leather objects, and that perennial favorite, shoes. Because you can't pick up everything, don't let your puppy wander around the house unsupervised. Keep him in a puppy-proof room or consider tethering him to your belt with a leash so he's always beside you. As an extra precaution, you can slather bitter-tasting products (available from your veterinarian or pet supply store) on objects you don't want your puppy to sample. Even spraying underarm deodorant on surfaces will dissuade most puppies from taking more than one lick.

But puppies are driven to chew, so you must give your puppy something acceptable to gnaw on. Choose chews carefully: no old shoes, no socks, no carpet remnants, nothing that resembles anything he could find around the house. What a puppy learns to chew on at an early age will tend to be what he looks for to chew on for the rest of his life. Only let your pup have a few chew toys at a time, rotating them every few days so he has the excitement of something new. Your choice of chews will depend on your dog's chewing power; some dogs chew with such gusto that they swallow big hunks, which can cause a potentially fatal impaction, while others have tender mouths and need smaller, softer chews. Rawhide, for example, is fine for some dogs, but others gulp down large hunks and can become very ill from it. Real bones can cause slab fractures of teeth that can bring hefty dental bills. Consider using the following:

- Interactive toys, such as those that can be filled with soft cheese, dog bones, or peanut butter. You can freeze them after filling to make them last even longer.
- Chew toys that can be soaked in water and frozen, providing relief for teething puppies.

Chewing can also result from boredom. Dogs, whether puppies or adults, can chew because there's nothing else to do. Most dogs do not get enough exercise, and since they can't watch television or read a book, they turn to their doggy entertainment center, which is too often your closet or new chair. Give your dog more exercise, both mental and physical. A sleeping dog can't chew. And again, be sure to provide him with more enticing acceptable things to chew on and play with.

Some cases of chewing don't stem from puppy impulses or boredom but from anxiety. Chewing that occurs when the dog is left alone, especially if it occurs around doors and windows or is accompanied by scratching and digging, may be a sign of separation anxiety. Such dogs are stressed about being left alone; they spend the time panting, drooling, and trying to find ways to escape and come find you. They also often urinate and defecate out of anxiety. Separation anxiety can occur in dogs of all ages. Punishing the dog only makes it worse; instead, work on a program of gradual desensitization to being left alone, leaving the dog for only a few minutes at a time. Talk to your veterinarian about other steps you can take.

Chewing is not just damaging; it's dangerous. Chewing electrical cords can lead to shocks and electrocution. Eating drugs and poisons has led to the deaths of many dogs. Although eating paper currency is an expensive habit, swallowing a single penny can be more expensive; unless it is removed, the penny may stay in the dog's stomach and release zinc, resulting in zinc poisoning. Swallowing stockings and socks can lead to intussusceptions, in which the intestines accordion upon themselves, requiring surgery. Prevention will save you money—and perhaps your puppy's life!

Australian Shepherd Development

His first year will bring incredible changes to your puppy, physically, behaviorally, and socially. Your role changes as he develops, and you need to know when he's old enough to train, for example, or what kind of play is best for his age. Here's what to expect from your puppy at different stages of development.

The Aussie Infant (Birth–Seven Weeks)

Physical Development

- His smell and taste are developed, but his eyes and ears are closed until almost 2 weeks of age.
- Teeth begin to emerge at 3 weeks of age, starting with canines (fangs). By 8 weeks, all 28 baby teeth are in.

Socialization

- For the first 3 weeks he prefers his dam to anyone.
- By 4 weeks he prefers his littermates. Playing with them teaches him to relate to other dogs and may be important for learning to inhibit his bites.

- Once people begin to feed him, he begins to attend more to them.
- By 7 weeks, he actively prefers people to his dam.

Behaviors

- He starts to eat semi-solid food by 3 weeks, and by 5 weeks is eating mostly solid food. The food he eats now will have a long-lasting influence on his adult preferences. If he eats only one food, he'll be cautious of novel foods. If he eats a variety, he'll prefer a variety.
- His dam no longer cleans up his wastes after he starts eating solid food. If he can, he'll totter away from his sleeping spot to do his duty. He's too young to learn housetraining concepts.
- By 7 weeks of age he's starting to be a little more cautious about new places and new things. He knows one person from another, and he prefers those he knows. He can learn simple commands.

Care and Experiences

- He needs to explore while he's still fearless. Good experiences at this age will stay with him throughout life, helping him take new situations in stride later on.
- It's a good idea if he has practice sleeping by himself for short stretches. A little crate or bed is perfect for learning to sleep alone, or with a cuddly warm toy.

Training

- As with human babies, early stimulation is vital for development.
- He can learn the concept of clicker training and some simple commands. The first commands he learns will tend to be his go-to commands for

the rest of his life; when he wants something, or is confused about what you want, he'll tend to go to these behaviors. Stick with the standards, like sitting.

- Try some simple leash training using a lightweight cat leash. Just put on the leash and let him lead you around. Then entice him a few feet in the direction you want to go by dangling a treat just in front of him. Give it to him when he walks there.

Play

- Be sure to introduce balls and other toys to him, as puppies learn specific play habits at an early age.

The Aussie Toddler (Eight–Twelve Weeks)

Physical Development

- All 28 of his baby teeth are in.
- His vision and hearing are almost adult-like, but not quite. They won't be fully mature until he's 10 weeks old.
- If he's a boy, both his testicles should be in his scrotum by now. If they're not, and he's destined for the show ring, it's time to consult with your veterinarian, as two normally descended testicles are required.

Socialization

- Starting at around 7 or 8 weeks, puppies gradually begin to become more fearful of novel situations until, by 12 weeks, they are more distrustful than trustful. That means you need to expose your puppy to as many situations as he'll encounter later in life as you can before this deadline.

Behaviors

- Bonding with his canine family reaches its highest point at 7 weeks of age. It will gradually decline until he's 10 weeks old, after which he will prefer you.

Care and Experiences

- After 9 weeks of age, puppies seem to cling to whatever substrate they learned to use for pottying between 7 and 9 weeks of age. Make sure that during this crucial time he's using whatever you want him to use for the rest of his life.
- Expose him to being alone for short periods. If you wait until he's 12 weeks old, studies have shown he will have a much more difficult time adjusting. Exposure should be for very short time periods, before he has a chance to become stressed.
- He should get his first puppy vaccinations at around 8 weeks.

Training

- He is eager to learn, and works well for either food or play.
- Now is the time to enroll him in puppy kindergarten class.

Play

- Introduce him to the concept of fetch. Puppies not exposed to fetch at an early age have difficulty understanding it later.

The Juvenile Aussie (Three–Six Months)

Physical Development

- At around 4 to 5 months his baby teeth start to be replaced by adult teeth. His small front teeth will fall out and be replaced by permanent teeth first, followed by his canine teeth and finally his rear teeth. Sometimes the baby canine teeth don't fall out and a new one comes in beside them. If they stay there for more than a few days or a week it could cause the new teeth to come in crooked and even adversely affect his occlusion, so you should consult your veterinarian.
- If you plan to neuter or spay your dog, the best time is at about 5 months of age, giving the dog time to mature but avoiding doing so

after sexual maturity. Spaying before the first estrus greatly reduces the chance of breast cancer later in life.

- He's getting more coordinated and much faster. He's also making one of the grandest discoveries of his short life: You can't catch him!

Socialization

- By 12 weeks of age his tendency to be cautious of new things has overwhelmed his tendency to be curious about them, and that tendency will increase for the next few months. This doesn't mean he should be sheltered. You need to continue exposing him to new people, places, and things, taking extra care to make sure he has good experiences. You may have to take things more slowly than you could have at a younger age.
- Social positions with any littermates gradually become more stable until the ranking order is fairly constant by week 16.

Behaviors

- His play is getting rougher, and he's using his mouth on everything. Handing him a toy often distracts him from chewing on you, but if not, do what his littermate would do when he plays too rough: say *"Ouch,"* and refuse to play until he calms down.
- He still objects to being separated from his family, whether canine or human. Keep giving him short periods alone. Studies have shown that soft stuffed toys, warm toys with a heartbeat, or a safe mirror can help alleviate his distress somewhat.

Care and Experiences

- It's time to do another home check to make sure your place is still puppy-proofed for this bigger, more adventurous dog.
- He's only now entering his heavy chewing stage. His baby teeth were capable of decorating everything with tiny pinprick holes, but his adult teeth can do a lot more damage.
- It's not unusual for him to regress when it comes to potty habits. Don't ask your 3-month-old pup to hold himself for more than three hours—or less, if he's been playing or drinking a lot.
- He will need additional puppy vaccinations, and he should get his rabies vaccination at about 16 weeks (or younger, depending on state law).

Training

- At no other time in your puppy's life is he more amenable to training, but by about 4 months of age the ease with which puppies learn starts to decline. Be sure you've introduced him to basic training concepts before then.
- He can easily learn how to sit, lie down, stay, come, and heel by 4 months of age. If you have aspirations to compete in advanced obedience or in agility, hunting, or trailing now's the time to start teaching him to climb over and under objects and to use his nose to seek out hidden objects.
- Now is the time to enroll him in an elementary puppy training class.

Play

- His games still center around play fighting, but you need to redirect his play to something more cooperative. Try some fetch; if he won't bring the ball back, practice in a hallway. Use two balls, stand midway down the hall, and throw one ball to one end. Once he gets it, encourage him to come back—use a treat if you have to—and when he gets to you, throw the other ball in the other direction. Keep it up until he knows his reward for bringing you one ball is the chance to chase another.
- He's ready for some more sophisticated toys. Puzzle and interactive toys that require him to work to get treats or other surprises out of them are great for occupying his mind when you can't be with him.

The Adolescent Aussie (Seven–Twelve Months)

Physical Development

- He's reached his adult size by now, although he still has some filling out to do.
- All 42 adult teeth should be in by 7 months. Any baby teeth remaining should have been examined by a veterinarian long ago. Always x-ray before pulling baby teeth, because not all dogs have permanent ones waiting to erupt in their place.
- Testicles should be permanently in place. If one or both testicles still haven't descended, talk to your veterinarian about what to do. At this age, the chance of them coming down is remote. It's not that they're not there; they're retained within his body, where the higher temperature renders them both incapable of creating viable sperm and more likely to become cancerous later in life. For this reason he'll probably need surgery to remove them.
- If not neutered or spayed, your Aussie is becoming sexually mature. If male, his testicles and penis are growing in size and he's showing interest in females in heat. He can probably sire puppies by 9 months of age. Females usually have their first estrus (heat, or season) between 6 and 10 months of age.

Socialization

- He's getting more sure of himself, maybe even cocky. But at around 8 to 9 months he undergoes a second fearful stage, when little negative experiences make a big impact on him. So continue to get him out and about, but with a watchful eye.

Behaviors

- He's still finding his place in the pack. Older dogs are now less tolerant of his transgressions. Keep an eye on them, but remember, the adult needs to lay down the rules to the youngster, and better now than later.
- He may try to push your limits, ignore your commands, and see what he can get away with. Deal with disobedience firmly, steering him toward more rewarding behaviors.
- Males that have not been castrated may start lifting their legs when they are 8 to 12 months of age, and some do it inside the house. This is a hard habit to break, and you absolutely must try to correct it early by watching him carefully and rushing him outside with a disapproving tone if you catch him in the act. A female may start to urinate more often as she comes into estrus and especially during estrus.
- He's reasoning more like an adult. Certain tests of memory and reasoning, such as "object permanence" (a test in which the dog detects that an object that was once there has been removed when he wasn't looking), show that dogs don't develop that ability until 8 or 9 months of age.

Care and Experiences

- It's time to update your puppy-proofing once again.
- He's going to need somewhat more exercise than before. He needs to walk around the block, sniff all the neat smells, and see something new every day.
- If he regresses in his housetraining, you need to take a step back in your training. He may look like an adult, but remember, he's been on this earth less than a year.

Training

- He really should know the basics—*sit, down, come, stay, heel*— by now. If you haven't yet enrolled in a class, it's time you did so he can practice around others. If he is getting bored with the basics, add some tricks or some of the advanced exercises. It's easier for him to learn them now, while he's still in the learning mode.
- If you have special plans for your dog, such as therapy work or search and rescue, it's time to join a group that can help you train him.

Play

- Try new, more complicated toys. Rotate them so it seems to him he's getting new toys every few days.
- A lot of his play now centers on showing you how much faster, stronger, and smarter he is than you. You can play along, but make sure you win or that you are the one to say when the game is over.

Puppy Nutrition

Your puppy's breeder may have suggested a brand of food he's already eating or even sent some home with you. If possible, stick with it for the first week or so of his time with you. He has enough to get used to without having a diet change. But you may eventually want to change to another diet, in which case you should know something about puppy food.

Commercial puppy foods identified by the words "complete and balanced nutrition for growing dogs based on American Association of Feed Control Officials (AAFCO) feeding trials" on the label are developed to be a puppy's sole diet. These foods do not require vitamin, mineral, or other supplements, and you can, in fact, throw off the balance of the diet by adding them. You should particularly avoid calcium, phosphorus, and vitamin D, as excesses may lead to developmental orthopedic diseases.

Recipes for homemade diets that provide balanced nutrition for puppies are also available, but it's important that such diets come from reputable sources. Check with your veterinarian to see if a proposed diet is reasonable.

FYI: Brain Food

Some studies have indicated that certain fatty acids are particularly important for early learning. One of these, docosahexaenoic acid (DHA), is an important component of the nervous system, including the brain and retina, and is critical for proper mental and visual function. Human infants fed DHA have better problem-solving abilities than do those not supplemented with DHA. Puppies appear to be the same. In fact, the level of DHA in puppies is partly dependent on their dam's level, especially during the last third of her pregnancy. Feeding the dam and, once weaned, puppies foods high in DHA can increase DHA levels in pups. Puppies with high DHA levels have been shown to perform better on several tests of learning and trainability compared with pups that were not supplemented with DHA. Commercial foods with DHA are available.

Breed Needs

Large Breed Food?

Most commercial puppy foods are designated for puppies of all sizes, but different-sized puppies actually have different requirements. Puppies of small- and medium-sized breeds can eat these foods, but puppies of large breeds (weighing more than 50 pounds [about 23 kilograms] as adults) should be fed a puppy food designed for large breeds. Aussies straddle this adult weight, so you may have to make an educated guess based on your puppy's sex (males are heavier than females) and the size of the parents. In fact, a good guideline is to assume your puppy will be the size of his same-sexed parent. Foods designed for large-breed puppies slow the rate of growth without affecting the final size of the dog. This slower rate of growth is important for decreasing developmental orthopedic diseases. It's not appropriate to feed adult maintenance food to large-breed puppies, as some people suggest; these foods are not formulated for growth and don't have the proper ratio of nutrients puppies need.

Most Aussie puppies aren't particular about their food, relishing pretty much anything you give them. When introducing a new food to your puppy, add it to the existing diet gradually over several days until it replaces the old in order to decrease the chance of gastrointestinal upset.

Puppies eat a lot for their size because they are growing. With young puppies you're usually safe to let them eat as much as they want at a meal. After 20 minutes, pick up the bowl. When possible, measure the food you give the puppy; otherwise watch the puppy's condition to make sure he is neither thin nor heavy.

Avoid free feeding, which encourages overeating and also makes it difficult for you to keep track of whether your puppy is off his feed. Puppies under the age of 6 months should be fed three or possibly four meals a day, changing to two to three times a day after six months. Small puppies (such as those of miniature Aussies) may need to eat more frequently. And don't forget the most vital nutrient: water! Keep a bowl of fresh water handy for your puppy at all times.

Puppy Veterinary Care

Whether your new puppy is from a breeder or a shelter, one of the first things you need to do is arrange a veterinary checkup within a couple of days of welcoming him home. This way, if the puppy has a preexisting condition, you can alert the breeder or shelter, especially if it's a contagious condition. Many breeder contracts insist on such an exam so that you both have assurance that the puppy is healthy at the time of transfer. And you'll want to know your puppy is starting off with a clean bill of health.

Before heading to the veterinarian, gather any previous health records, including details of vaccinations and deworming. Write down what you're feeding in case the veterinarian asks. Also record any questions, possible signs of illness, or problems you're having with your new pet so that you don't forget them once in the exam room. If you have pet health insurance, bring the information for it. Bring a fresh stool sample (not the whole thing; about a tablespoon is ample).

Once at the clinic, leave the puppy in his crate or hold him on your lap. Don't let him visit with other dogs, who may not feel well. Don't let him on the floor because of the risk of communicable diseases in an unvaccinated puppy. If he's too large to crate or hold, bring a towel for him to sit on.

Puppy Vaccinations

Your puppy received his early immunity through his dam's colostrum during the first few days of nursing. As long as your puppy still has that immunity, he will be immune to the diseases his dam is immune to. That's one reason it's important for the dam to be up to date on her vaccinations before she's bred. While your puppy is covered by the immunity he received from his dam, any vaccinations you give him won't provide sufficient immunity. But after several weeks this maternal immunity begins to decrease. As it does, both the chance of a vaccination being effective and the chance of getting a communicable disease (if unprotected) rise. The problem is that immunity diminishes at different ages in different dogs. So starting at around 6 to 8 weeks of age, a series of vaccinations is given in order to leave as little unprotected time as possible. During this time of uncertainty it's best not to take your puppy around places where unvaccinated dogs may congregate. Deadly viruses, such as parvovirus, can remain in the soil for months after an infected dog has shed virus in its feces there. Timely vaccination is imperative for puppies to remain protected against disease. For a few at-risk puppies, such as orphans or those exposed to parvovirus, some veterinarians suggest giving the first vaccination as early as 5 weeks of age. But for most puppies, the first vaccination should be given between 6 and 8 weeks of age, a second dose between 9 and 11 weeks, and a third dose between 12 and 14 weeks. Rabies vaccination is given between 12 and 16 weeks of age. Vaccinations should be given at least three weeks apart; when given closer together, the second vaccine may not be effective.

Vaccination is a medical procedure and, as such, is not one-size-fits-all. Vaccines are divided into core vaccines, which are advisable for all dogs, and non-core vaccines, which are advisable only for some dogs. Core vaccines are those for rabies, distemper, canine parvovirus, and hepatitis (using the CAV-2 vaccine, not the CAV-1, which can cause adverse reactions

FYI: Spay/Neuter Considerations

There are long-term health pros and cons for both spaying and neutering. For females, spaying before the first heat greatly decreases the risk of breast cancer. This is the most common tumor of female dogs. Spaying also removes the possibility of pyometra, a potentially fatal infection of the uterus. In a spay, the uterus is removed, also removing the chance of pyometra.

Spaying has a few health cons, however. It may be associated with an increased risk of anterior cruciate ligament injury— a torn ligament in the knee joint that is seen mostly in large dogs. Spaying is also associated with an increased risk of urinary incontinence, which occurs in 5 to 20 percent of spayed females, more commonly in large breeds. It may also be associated with a slightly greater rate of bone cancer and hemangiosarcoma (a cancer of the blood vessels). While bone cancer is not common in Aussies, hemangiosarcoma is the most common cancer in Aussies.

The choice to spay should be made on a case-by-case basis. For most dogs, the convenience and the health benefits probably outweigh the health risks. For large dogs especially, it is not a good idea to spay at an extremely young age. Overall, it is probably best to spay bitches between 3 months of age and their first heat— sometime around 4 to 5 months of age.

With castration (neutering), there are also pros and cons. Castration removes the risk of testicular cancer. It reduces the risk of an enlarged prostate, which occurs in about 80 percent of intact male dogs over the age of 6 years. The condition can be treated with (among other things) castration.

Castration has some cons, though. Like spaying, it may be associated with an increased risk of anterior cruciate ligament injuries, and with a slightly greater rate of bone cancer and hemangiosarcoma, both more common in larger breeds. It's also been associated with a slightly higher risk of prostate cancer.

Like spaying, castration should be decided on a case-by-case basis. Many dog parks, doggy daycares, and camps won't allow dogs that have not been castrated to attend. If you castrate your dog, you should probably have it done around 6 months of age, before he starts urine marking. Once that becomes a habit, he may continue to mark even after castration.

but is still sold by some feed stores). Non-core vaccines include those for leptospirosis, bordetella, parainfluenza, and Lyme disease. Your veterinarian can advise you if your dog's lifestyle and environment put him at risk for these diseases. Remember, more is not necessarily better!

Although adverse reactions are uncommon, some vaccines are more likely to cause them than others, and such reactions are more common in young puppies. Because leptospirosis has a comparatively high rate of adverse reactions in puppies, it is usually not advisable for them. If reactions to vaccines do occur, they usually happen within the day or two following administration and consist of a low-grade fever, lethargy, and loss of appetite. Less commonly, severe reactions such as hives, facial swelling, or vomiting may occur.

Most vaccinations are combined so that only one injection needs to be given. A "five-way" vaccine, for example, usually includes distemper, parvovirus, adenovirus, hepatitis, and parainfluenza. Although it's possible to administer your own vaccinations, it's prudent to have a veterinarian do so. The veterinarian knows which vaccines are advisable in your area; not all vaccine is equal, and vaccine acquired elsewhere may not have been stored properly. Rabies vaccine must be administered by a veterinarian for legal reasons in case your dog bites someone.

Spaying and Neutering

As your puppy grows up, one of the decisions you'll be faced with is when—or if—to spay or neuter your dog. Before deciding to breed, you should realize that having a litter of puppies entails some risk to the dam—and considerable expense and work for you. As a responsible dog owner, you won't want to add to the overpopulation of dogs. You'll need to decide if you meet the requirements for a good breeder that you looked for when you were searching for a dog. These include health testing, buyer screening, and the ability to take back any dogs you produce if their owners cannot keep them.

Even though you may be adamant that you can keep your dog from having an unplanned litter, it takes diligence and security measures to ensure a mating does not take place. Living with a dog in heat can be difficult. Most dogs go into heat twice a year; it lasts about three weeks, during which time she has a bloody discharge that can stain your rugs and furniture. You can place britches on her, but she will often pull the britches off. Some females will escape from the yard if left unsupervised, going in search of a male. Other times, a male will break into the yard—or stand vigil outside your door. If you own both an intact male and female, the male may drive you crazy with his panting and whining. Many owners opt to board their females during heat, but this entails extra costs. Spaying is definitely the convenient choice.

Intact males tend to roam in search of females, and they are more likely to fight with other male dogs. They are very likely to urine mark inside the house. Again, castration is the convenient option.

Both surgeries are very safe, although as with any surgery, some slight risk is involved. Spaying (ovariohysterectomy) is more involved. The veterinarian will place a small incision in the abdomen and remove the ovaries and uterus through it. In castration, the veterinarian will remove the testicles, leaving the scrotal sack, which will shrink and disappear. If a dog has one or both testicles undescended, the veterinarian will have to place an incision in the abdomen and remove them that way.

Note that spayed or neutered dogs cannot compete in conformation shows, but they can compete in all other events. For most dog owners, however, spaying and neutering is the best choice for their pets. Your life will be easier, and your dog's life will be simpler, without the stress of unrequited love.

Chapter Five

Living with an Australian Shepherd

A ustralian Shepherds are good at many jobs, but the job they're best at is being your companion. Give them a chance, and they'll be at your side whether you're indoors or out, working or lounging, laughing or crying. Your Aussie will be both friend and family member, but like any new friends, you'll both have to learn something about one another to make the best of your partnership.

Understanding Your Aussie

People and dogs are surprisingly good at interpreting one another's body language. Some scientists believe that the domestication process has enabled some dogs to decipher human body language. Dogs seem to be able to understand that pointing or staring at something means to follow the direction of the finger or gaze, an ability wolves don't have. In fact, it appears that only some breeds of dogs have this ability. Fortunately, this includes most herding breeds.

But how good are you at interpreting your dog's body language? If your dog yawns, licks his lips, or shakes himself off, you have a good idea what it means—or do you? Yawning could mean he's tired—or it could mean he's nervous. Licking his lips could mean he's hungry—or it could mean he's uneasy. Shaking himself off could mean he's wet—or it could mean he's relieved. Here's a quick rundown on what your Aussie's body language is saying.

Behavior Challenges

As many as 90 percent of all dog owners report some behavioral problem with their dogs. Fortunately, that number is almost certainly much lower among Aussie owners. Some of the more common Aussie complaints are hyperactivity, shyness, fearful behavior, barking, nipping, aggression, and separation anxiety. In many cases, you can help your dog get over these problems by means of training books or classes, or your veterinarian's

PERSONALITY POINTERS
Australian Shepherd Body Language

Aussie Mood	Friendliness	Interest or Excitement	Playfulness	Pleasure	Confidence
Stance	Advancing, relaxed	Leaning forward	Active, advancing	Relaxed	Facing squarely; standing sideways
Posture	Leaning forward	Leaning forward	Body lowered on front end only	Body upside down and rolling	Leaning forward; head held high, arched neck
Tail*	Wagging	Wagging slowly and broadly	Wagging slowly but broadly	Wagging slowly and broadly or quickly and broadly	High
Ears	Forward or relaxed	Pricked and forward	Pricked and forward		Forward
Eyes		Dilated pupils	Dilated pupils, wide		Relaxed
Mouth			Open with lip corner pulled upward, often tongue showing; biting		

*Most Aussies don't have a tail, but a wagging rump usually means a wagging tail, and a tucked rump a tucked tail. You can also get a clue from the tail nub.

Apprehension or Anxiety	Submission	Fear	Aggression	Dominance
Retreating	Retreating, freezing	Retreating	Advancing; facing squarely	Advancing; facing squarely
Body or head lowered	Leaning backward; body or head lowered (and/or twisted); body twisted upside down; head turned away	Leaning backward; body or head lowered; body twisted upside down	Leaning forward with stiff-legged stance	Leaning forward with stiff-legged stance
Tucked	Tucked but wagging; wagging quickly and broadly	Tucked	Raised, held stiffly, and quivering	Raised, held stiffly, and quivering
	Down	Back	Pricked and forward	Pricked and forward
Blinking rapidly	Turned away and squinting	Dilated pupils	Open wide and staring; dilated pupils	
Licking lips; yawning; panting (may also indicate pain)	Licking the air toward you or another dog; front teeth showing, with no signs of aggression; muzzle push	Slightly open with lip corner pulled back, all teeth showing; biting	Agape with lip corner forward; face, nose, or lips wrinkled, teeth showing; biting	

FYI: Spite and Guilt

The first step in choosing how to treat your dog's behavior problem is finding out what is causing it. Your dog's behaviors are the result of his inborn inclinations, his experiences, and his developmental maturity. One cause of unwanted behavior you should immediately discard as a possibility is spite. As far as we know, dogs do not have the capacity to plan something out of spite. Nor do dogs have the capacity to feel guilt. What owners interpret as a guilty look is almost always a worried and submissive look. Remove the words "spite" and "guilt" from your vocabulary when it comes to dog behavior.

advice. Not all trainers are good with behavior problems; look for a trainer who is a member of the Association of Pet Dog Trainers (*www.apdt.com*) and certified through the Certification Council for Professional Dog Trainers (*www.ccpdt.org*). In some cases, especially in cases of aggression toward people, you may do better to seek the help of a veterinary behaviorist, a specialist with extensive training in pet behavior. Your veterinarian can consult with one or refer you to one in your area (go to *www.dacvb.org* or a listing). Clinical behaviorists are trained in diagnostics and treatment, and have the advantage of being able to recognize and treat organic problems such as brain tumors, epilepsy, and chemical imbalances that may be responsible for behavior problems. They are keen observers of behavior and may spot clues that you have either missed or misinterpreted. They can prescribe drugs that can help alongside training.

Hyperactivity

In most cases, hyperactivity is really a case of underactivity. Aussies have to be active in order to do the job they were bred to do—which was not to sit in a house all day waiting for you to come home from work. Aussies need mental, physical, and social stimulation. When they lack any of these they will try to make up for them any way they can, which often translates to hyperactivity and poor behavior. A dog lacking social stimulation may throw himself at his owner when he finally has the chance to interact, licking and jumping and making such a pest of himself in his quest for attention that his owner labels him as hyperactive and banishes him to the yard, crate, or garage. A dog lacking physical stimulation may run helter-skelter when he finally has the chance, again prompting his owner to lock him back up. A dog lacking mental stimulation may get into all sorts of mischief when he finally has access to an interesting environment, causing his owner to label him destructive and put him back where there's nothing at all he can do. This cycle of isolation and unruly behavior tends to weaken the bonding of the person to the dog, ultimately leading to the dog's relinquishment to

a shelter. Crating and confinement may subdue unwanted behavior, but it won't help the dog get better.

Remember, chances are your Aussie is not hyperactive but simply needs more exercise than you provide him. That means the solution is exercise, both mental and physical. Teach him tricks. Make them challenging. Jogging, games, and exercise can tire your dog physically, which is half (but only half) the battle. Canine sports such as agility and Flyball combine mental challenges with physical ones. Tracking is also a good outlet. Herding is the very best outlet.

Don't expect your dog to be calm without first working off some of his energy, but even then, he needs to be rewarded for calm behavior. Speak calmly and quietly. Ignore his pushy or overactive behavior. Reward him for sitting or lying down and staying, and for being calm as you gently pet and massage him. But first make sure he's had enough exercise to fully appreciate the comfort of relaxation.

Barking

Barking is handy when it comes to warning of intruders or pushing a recalcitrant steer on his way, which is why barking comes naturally to Aussies. But that doesn't mean they have to drive you crazy at home. Most Aussies bark out of excitement, announcing a person at the door or a cat on the fence. But some also bark at anything, to the point of being annoying. If you have an excitement barker, you need to teach him that being quiet is more rewarding that barking. Wait until he is quiet momentarily and then give him a treat. This may be easier if you have him sit and stay first. Keep repeating this, gradually increasing how long he must be quiet before getting a treat. Add a cue word, such as "*Shhhhh*" as you start your timing. Eventually he learns that "*Shhhhh*" means that if he is quiet he will get a treat. Next check on him randomly and if he is being quiet when you do, give him a treat. Don't give him one if he is barking.

Don't yell at your dog to make him stop barking. He'll only think you are joining in the fun. Be calm and quiet yourself. If need be you can throw a noisy can on the ground to stop him momentarily so he can be quiet enough to begin training.

Some Aussies are boredom barkers. They have nothing else to do but bark, bark, bark. The solution is obvious: Give them something to do. Give them interactive toys, even another dog, and make sure they're well exercised, mentally and physically. Some bark from loneliness; their reward is you coming out to tell them to be quiet. That solution, too, is obvious:

PERSONALITY POINTERS

Recognizing the Bite

Playful biting	Fearful biting	Aggressive biting
Wagging tail (rump)	Tucked tail (rump)	Stiffly held tail (if present)
Bowing position	Crouched position	Stiff, tiptoe position
Running and bouncing	Slinking or cornered	Standing or charging
Barks and growls together	Whines and growls	Low growl, perhaps barks
Breathy exhale sounds	No such sounds	No such sounds
Mouthing	No mouthing	No mouthing
Eye contact	Looks away	Eye contact
Licks at you	Licks own lips	No licking
Lip corner pulled upward	Lip corner pulled back	Lip corner pulled forward
Repeated nips or grabs	Sudden bite, then retreat	Sudden hard bites

Bring him in to socialize before he starts barking. If he's already barking, wait until he's quiet before letting him in.

Nipping and Aggression

Nipping is a common behavior of Aussie puppies, who may use it, along with barking and blocking your path, to try to herd you about. For solutions to puppy nipping, see page 50. Whereas most nipping tends to be playful, some Aussie nips and bites can stem from aggressive and potentially dangerous behavior. Some people, however, misinterpret playful behavior for aggression. Dogs bite for many reasons, including feeling threatened, guarding their territory or belongings, scrapping with other dogs, or challenging your authority. Be sure you know why your Aussie is biting.

Dog aggression is not a single entity. Clinical behaviorists have categorized canine aggression into various types. Identifying the type of aggression requires astute observation; proper identification is needed before choosing a course of treatment. For almost all cases of aggression directed toward people, you are better off getting professional help rather than tackling the problem on your own. Some of the major categories include

- **Playful aggression:** inappropriately rough play that may get carried away, resulting in actual growls and nips.
- **Pain aggression:** response to pain or the threat of pain, often by grabbing a hand; may be responsible for some cases of biting rough children.

- **Fear aggression:** response to threat of attack, pain, inappropriate punishment, or inappropriately perceived threat. The dog may bark, snarl, tremble, cower, and retreat. Bites are especially likely if the dog is cornered, but may also occur from behind.
- **Redirected aggression:** aggression toward someone who was not part of the original interactions, such as purposefully biting a person who intervenes in a dog fight.
- **Interdog aggression:** usually occurs within same-sex pairs in socially mature dogs.
- **Predatory aggression:** silent stalking and chasing of animals and sometimes small humans, especially those who squeal, flee, and act unpredictably.
- **Territorial aggression:** protection of yard, car, house, or kennel, and especially any property in which boundaries are clearly defined, such as with a fence.
- **Protective aggression:** protection of one or more family members by standing between, barking, growling, and biting when another person approaches or makes quick movements.
- **Maternal aggression:** hormonally controlled protection of puppies, toys, or nest when nursing or in pseudopregnancy.
- **Possessive aggression:** trying to obtain or refusing to relinquish toys or stolen household objects; growling and possibly biting if somebody attempts to take them.
- **Food-related aggression:** protecting food, treats, and bones from people and other dogs; growling or biting at perceived threats to possession of the food.

- **Dominance aggression:** controlling, threatening, or biting people who the dog perceives to challenge or attempt to control him.
- **Idiopathic aggression:** full aggressive display that appears to occur suddenly out of context.

Some of the more common types of aggressive behavior will be discussed below. In all cases, the information given here for treatment is not meant as a substitute for the diagnosis and advice of a clinical behaviorist who can see your dog in the flesh.

Fearfulness

Aussies are a naturally bold breed, but like all dogs, some can develop irrational fears. Living in fear robs you and your dog from engaging in lots of normal fun activities and puts your dog at risk for panic running, fear-biting, and high stress levels. Left untreated, fear problems tend to get worse. Common fears are fears of strange people, strange dogs, thunder, or gunshots. Helping your dog overcome his fear uses similar concepts no matter what the feared object or situation.

The Aussie's naturally wary temperament can sometimes become overly wary, especially if the dog does not receive adequate socialization when young. An overly wary Aussie can become shy of strangers. Some can even become aggressive toward strangers if they feel they cannot otherwise escape from them. The best cure is prevention by means of extensive socialization when young and continuing throughout life. Shy adults can get better, but only if you approach therapy as a long-term and ongoing process rather than something you can accomplish in just a few weeks.

Breed Truths

Aggression Myths

"Scruff shakes are good corrections because they mimic the way a mother dog corrects her puppies." *Not true.* In fact, mother dogs rarely, if ever, correct their pups by scruff shaking, nor do other dogs commonly correct each other that way.

"Alpha rolls are good corrections because they mimic the way a dominant dog exerts his dominance over a subordinate dog." *Not true.* In fact, dominant dogs exert most of their dominance simply by ignoring subordinates, much as a celebrity might ignore the masses. Alpha rolls conducted by humans in attempts to subdue an already challenging dog often result in dog bites.

The old practice of flooding a shy or fearful dog with whatever it is he is afraid of while preventing him from escaping typically doesn't work for a couple of reasons. First, the dog's lack of control over the situation makes him even more fearful. Dogs with a history of being able to exert control over their own lives tend to be more confident and more resistant to fear than dogs without such a history. Second, flooding depends on the dog becoming so habituated to the fearful stimulus that he can no longer maintain his level of fearfulness. Most dogs never achieve this, and end up being even more scared of the situation.

A better way to cope with fears is to use a system of gradual desensitization. You need to help your dog build his confidence and feeling of control. Your goal is to start each training session at a level that may cause some anxiety to your dog, but not so much that the dog is still fearful at that level at the end of the session. Remember, your dog is learning to be calm. If he's still afraid at the end of a session, all you have taught him is how to be scared. You can help him learn to be calm by combining several behavioral techniques.

- Prevent him from escaping on his own, but give him a way to earn his way to a point farther from the thing that's scaring him. For example, if he does a trick you can then walk him away from the scary thing for a minute.
- Have him do something incompatible with fearful behavior, such as herding, playing, or eating.
- Be sure he can't cue off your nervousness, or another dog's. Don't clutch him to you, pull on the leash, or coddle him when he acts fearful. Instead, if something startling happens, act as though it's funny; if a stranger appears, act like you're glad.
- Ask your veterinarian about antianxiety drugs that can help during training.

Separation Distress

Separation distress is a normal behavior in young dogs. Under natural circumstances, separation from the dam and littermates would be a gradual process, allowing the youngster to adjust. In domestic dogs, it's more often an abrupt process, beginning when the puppy goes to his new home. The dog can become scared very easily when first left alone and can quickly come to expect to feel afraid when by himself. When that happens, the situation builds on itself and works up to full-blown separation distress.

Signs of a dog with separation distress include whining, howling, barking, panting, drooling, pacing, and digging or chewing at doors and windows while you're gone. The dog may also have urinated and defecated on the floor or in the crate. Many people think the dog is spiting them, but dogs never destroy out of spite. The fact that your dog may look guilty when you come home usually stems from past experiences with what seems to him to be your irrational homecoming behavior. Here he is finally reunited with his loved one and you start acting crazy. He learns to act submissive when you return home, especially if the house just happens to be in shambles.

If you're still not convinced, set up a video camera and watch him while you're gone. You won't see a dog gleefully venting his anger on your home. You'll see a dog that is upset and perhaps near panicked. This is not a dog that needs to be punished; he's a dog that needs to be helped. Start with these steps:

- **Downplay departures:** Minimize any cues that you're leaving. Don't turn the radio or television on or off reliably, don't rattle keys, don't put your shoes on right before you leave, and don't have any big good-bye scenes.
- **Gradually lengthen time alone:** Leave for only short periods at first—maybe 30 seconds. Your goal is to return before your dog has a chance to get upset. Work up to longer times gradually, repeating each level several times before moving to a longer period of absence.
- **Use a safety cue:** When first training with short periods, give your dog a cue that says to him, "I'll be right back." You can spray some air freshener in the room, turn on a radio (if you don't usually have one on), or put down a special bed. You want him to associate the safety cue with feeling calm. If you must be gone longer than your dog can tolerate, don't give him the safety cue.
- **Downplay returns:** Just as you downplayed your departure, return as though it was no big deal. That means no crazed reunions. Ignore your dog until he is calm, or better, give him a cue to sit or do some other behavior involving self-control, and then reward him for that.
- **Consider antianxiety aids:** Many dogs may not be calm enough in your absence to make much progress. The use of dog-appeasing phero-mones, which are odors that mimic the calming scent of a lactating dam, has been shown to help some dogs. They are available from pet stores as a spray or room plug-in. Your veterinarian may also consider prescribing antianxiety drugs during training.

The best time to deal with separation distress is before it ever happens, when your dog is a puppy. Begin by leaving him for very short periods, perhaps with a special treat or interactive toy. If you do have a dog with separation distress, consult your veterinarian or, better yet, a veterinary behaviorist to deal with the problem. It can be fixed, but the sooner you start, the easier it will be.

Exercising Your Aussie

You've heard over and over how you must exercise your Aussie's mind and body, but you may still be wondering exactly how to accomplish it. Although dog sports such as herding, Flyball, and agility are great means of flexing your Aussie's mental and physical muscles, for the average person it's a lot more practical to take your dog running, hiking, or playing.

Walking and Jogging

Walking your Aussie is a start—but it's only a start. Keep up a brisk pace and increase your own endurance to a couple of miles. Jogging is better, but depending on your Aussie's condition, he may have to work up to it. Don't jog a puppy or otherwise force him to do more than he wants to on his own,

BE PREPARED! Weather Warnings

Aussies deal well with cold weather but not as well with warm weather. Be very careful not to exercise your Aussie in the heat of the day. Dogs can't cool themselves as well as people can, and heatstroke can claim their lives far too easily.

Don't take your dog for long summer hikes, and don't leave him in the yard without shade, water, and ventilation. Consider adding a shallow wading pool to his yard accessories. If you have a real swimming pool, take the time to teach him to swim and to find where the pool steps are. If there are no steps, you can buy a floating platform for him to climb up on.

Dogs, especially light-skinned dogs, can get sunburn and melanoma. If your dog likes to sun worship, rub a sunblock on his belly and the top of his nose, the most common sites of problems.

as the pounding and stress on his joints could damage them. When jogging, try to run on softer ground rather than hard pavement. Especially avoid pavement on hot afternoons; even though the air temperature may have fallen, pavement often remains very hot. Check the dog's foot pads regularly for blistering, peeling, and cracks. Always bring plenty of water with you, and a cell phone in case either of you needs someone from home to come get you! With regular conditioning your Aussie should be able to run 5 or even 10 miles without a problem.

Although retractable leashes are very handy for walking, take care that you don't enable your dog to relieve himself in neighborhood yards or suddenly run into the road and the path of a car. Keep an eye out for loose dogs; in fact, it's a good idea to carry pepper spray in case your dog should be attacked. Of course, don't let your dog chase cats or other neighborhood dogs.

Hiking

Taking to the wilds for a hike is even higher on the list of Aussie adventures than walking or jogging. Ideally, you should keep your dog on a leash when hiking. In fact, many parks require it. Loose dogs can chase wildlife, threaten other hikers, and endanger horseback riders. They can also become victims of unforeseen dangers themselves. Not only do Aussies scamper about with little regard for their safety, but dog paws lack the grasping ability of human hands, and once they begin to slip they can do little to stop themselves. Dogs die every year from falling off cliffs or mountainsides. To make things worse, mountain and foothill areas may be home to abandoned mine shafts and their air vents.

Although your Aussie may think he can best any wild animal, a few animals can get the better of him. Porcupines, skunks, raccoons, badgers, cougars, coyotes, and bears are just a sampling of the wildlife you don't want your Aussie to confront. Poisonous snakes, especially rattlesnakes, are high on most people's lists of dreaded animals encountered in the wild. Their preferred habitats vary widely between species, but most prefer drier areas, often retreating in burrows, dense vegetation, hollow logs, or rock outcroppings. You may be able to find a rattlesnake prevention clinic, often sponsored by hunting dog clubs, that teaches your dog to avoid rattlesnakes in one lesson. The giant marine toad of south Florida (as well as extreme south Texas) is typically 4–10 inches (about 10–25 cm) long and is primarily nocturnal. It secretes a toxic substance from the large paratoid glands behind its eyes that can burn eyes and sicken dogs, even proving fatal to small dogs and puppies.

And one more warning: Although dogs don't get reactions to poison ivy or poison oak, your dog can carry the irritants on his fur and transmit them to you when you rub him. Keep your dog away from these plants for your own good!

Swimming

Most Aussies take to water naturally, but they should still be introduced gradually. Look for shallow water your Aussie can run through, like a big puddle. Gradually encourage him to go a bit deeper. You may need to throw something for him to retrieve or simply go in with him. If he thrashes around in the water once he's over his head, chances are his front end is too high compared to his rear end. Just lift his rear up so his front legs don't break the surface of the water, and he'll be swimming in no time!

Be aware that even the best swimming dog can't overcome strong surf or undertow. If a sign says swimming is unsafe for people, it is unsafe for dogs as well. Normally placid creeks can swell into killer torrents from upstream rain, especially those in desert regions. Many ditches have steep banks or bulkheads that dogs cannot climb. The aqueducts of southern California have drowned many a dog. Cold northern waters pose special hazards. Hypothermic dogs can lose the ability to swim with the strength necessary to make it back to shore. Dogs can break through thin ice. Ice that breaks under a dog's weight will almost certainly not support yours, making rescue dangerous or impossible.

Along the shoreline, make sure your Aussie isn't eating bait (which could contain fish hooks) or any dead fish. In the American Northwest dogs can get so-called salmon poisoning from eating raw salmon, steelhead, trout, and some other species that are infected with small flukes, which in turn contain *Neorickettsia helminthoeca*. A few days to weeks after eating the infected fish, the dog gets progressively sicker. Left untreated, most dogs die within two weeks. Don't forget that your dog may not be the only animal in the water. The cottonmouth, or water moccasin, lives in swamps, lakes, rivers, and ditches. Even more widespread is the snapping turtle. Snappers are aggressive and have bitten body parts off of curious dogs with their sharp beaks. The largest freshwater threat is the alligator, which considers dogs an irresistible delicacy.

The smallest freshwater threat comes from creatures you can't even see. Giardia is a microscopic organism found in many water sources. When your Aussie drinks that seemingly pristine water straight from nature, he may ingest giardia and become ill sometime later with stomach cramps and loose stools. Avoid any water that has a peculiar odor, color, or surface oiliness, or that is obviously fed by runoff from polluted areas.

Swimming pools are one of the safest places your Aussie can swim. Just make sure he knows where the steps are so he can get out by himself.

Backyard Games

Aussies will jump at the chance to partake in just about any game, but disc (Frisbee) catching is one of their very favorites. It does have drawbacks, however. The Aussie's addictive personality means that he will never tire of the game. Even when your throwing arm is aching, he will still be shoving a disc at your hands. Indoors, you may have to hide the disc if you don't want it crammed in your lap every few minutes, accompanied by expectant eyes upon you. Disc catching can have some health repercussions, too. Many Aussies excel in jumping and twisting to catch the disc—but that sort of gymnastics can cause injuries, especially of the spine and the knees' cruciate ligaments. In addition, repeatedly catching a hard plastic disc can wear down and even break teeth. For these reasons, teach your Aussie a "game over" word, and once you say the word, don't give in; don't encourage somersaults or giant leaps; and use a soft flexible disc made just for dogs.

To teach your dog to catch a disc, get him interested in it by playing keep-away or tug, or by throwing it and playing fetch. Then hold it up so he has to jump for it. Once he's doing that, throw it a few feet forward as he jumps, still close enough so he can catch it. Keep extending the distance he has to go for it. You can also throw it toward him—but not directly at him. Throw it past him, so he can jump for it as it flies by. It will take some practice, but Aussies catch on to the game quickly.

You can play lots of games in your yard, including such standards as fetch, keep-away, and tug. You can also practice some of the fundamentals of tracking by having your dog follow your scent trail to find hidden objects inside and outside the house. Have him watch you hide an object, then let him go find it. Use a cue like *"Find it!"* so he knows to start looking. Gradually hide the object better, and do it when he can't see where you put it. He'll quickly learn that he can follow your scent to the treasure. Just make sure you don't confuse him with crossing scent trails.

You can also practice some agility basics for fun. Set up a few jumps made of PVC pipes or simply brooms set across cinderblocks. You can buy a child's play tunnel and use it. If you have access to straw bales, set them up as a climbing area. Your Aussie will love running through the obstacle course!

Traveling with Your Aussie

Aussies are great travel companions: calm enough to travel quietly, active enough to enjoy excursions to see the sights, and protective enough to make you feel a little more secure. But taking any dog on a car trip requires some planning. You'll need to find motels that allow dogs, and you'll need to make plans for keeping him safe and comfortable when you stop to eat, shop, or sightsee.

Car Safety

You'll be wearing a seatbelt while you drive and your Aussie should have the equivalent: a crate that's secured to the car. Otherwise, if you slam on brakes or have an accident, your dog can become a flying missile, striking you or the dashboard, or even being ejected from the car. As an extra safety measure, place emergency information on the side of the crate that says something like, "In case of emergency, take this dog to a veterinarian, then contact the following persons (and list their contact information). Payment of all expenses incurred is guaranteed (include a signed consent form, or

an emergency contact who can provide a credit card number)." Note any medications or health problems your dog may have. Remember, you may not always be able to speak for your dog after an accident.

Of course, your dog should be wearing identification as well, and not just your home phone number. If you're on vacation, add a contact number of someone back home or where you can be reached.

When traveling alone, be sure you have a way to keep your dog cool should you have to run inside a rest stop to relieve yourself. This may mean bringing an extra set of keys so that you can keep the air conditioning running, or locking him in a crate, locking the crate in the car, and leaving a window open along with a battery-operated fan. Ice packs—or better, one of the cooling pads made for dogs using water-retaining gel pellets—can also help keep things cool. But don't rely on such measures for any longer than it takes you to hurry to the bathroom and back.

Despite all the warnings about leaving dogs in cars in summer heat, many dogs die every year from just that. Studies show that the temperature inside cars can heat to lethal temperatures within 30 minutes, even if the weather outside is relatively cool. Regardless of outside air temperature, cars heat up at a similar rate—gaining 80 percent of their final temperature within 30 minutes. Cars that start at a comfortable 72°F (22°C), for example, soar to a deadly 117°F (47°C) after 60 minutes in the sun. Cracking the windows scarcely affects the temperature inside.

Helpful Hints

Online Travel Resources

www.1clickpethotels.com
www.aaa.com
www.canineauto.com
www.dogfriendly.com
www.doggonefun.com
www.fidofriendly.com
www.petsonthego.com
www.takeyourpet.com
www.travelpet.com
www.travelpets.com

Lodging

Many motels allow well-mannered pets, but their numbers are decreasing as more dog owners abuse the privilege. To keep pets welcome, be sure to follow these rules:

- Bring his crate, or at least his own dog bed, in the room with you. If he gets on the bed, bring a sheet or roll down the bedspread so he doesn't get hair on it.
- Never leave your dog unattended in the room. He could feel deserted and try to dig his way out the door, or simply bark the whole time.
- If he has an accident on the carpet, don't try to hide it. Clean what you can and tell the management. Leave a big tip for housecleaning.
- Don't wash food bowls in the sink. The food clogs the drain.
- Clean up any poop your dog deposits on the grounds.
- Be considerate of others. Don't let him bark!

Communicating with Your Australian Shepherd _____

Your Aussie actually sees, hears, smells, and tastes a different world than you do. That difference in sensory ability is one thing that makes dogs so useful to people, but it is also sometimes very confusing. Understanding your Aussie's sensory world can help you understand why sometimes you may have a failure to communicate.

Scent   The biggest difference is in the sense of smell. While humans are visually oriented, dogs are smell oriented. Although not bred for their scenting abilities, Aussies can tell people apart through scent and can follow a human trail. Many Aussies have earned AKC tracking titles, or Utility obedience titles that require the dog to detect an object his handler has touched. Dogs trail people and other animals by scenting microscopic rafts of skin that fall to the ground, as well as the scent of their clothes, makeup, exhaled air, and even what they've eaten. They also detect crushed vegetation and stirred-up dirt from each footstep.

Like all dogs, Aussies use their sense of smell in social interactions. They get to know each other by first sniffing at each other's genitals, anus, mouth corners, and ears, all areas that produce a good deal of scent. This is also why dogs tend to head for the most embarrassing places on people to sniff!

Dogs leave powerful scent signals through anal sac secretions. Some of these secretions are forced out whenever the dog defecates, imparting extra, and presumably individualized, scent to the feces. When dogs are extremely frightened, they expel their anal sacs to produce a strong musky smell that instantly elicits intense interest from other dogs, perhaps telling them that something frightening happened there.

Dogs also get information about other dogs from the urine they leave. They may even lick some of it up in order to sample it with their vomeronasal organ, a small organ in the roof of the mouth used to decide if females are in estrus.

Hearing   Your Aussie can hear mid-range noises about four times farther away than you can. He can also hear high-pitched sounds you can't hear at any distance. The lowest-pitched sounds that dogs and people can hear are about the same, around 45 to 65 hertz (Hz). However, people hear sounds of around 3,000 Hz most easily (most people's voices are near that frequency), but dogs are most sensitive to higher-pitched sounds of around 8,000 Hz. The highest pitch that people can hear is 23,000 Hz; dogs can hear up to 45,000 Hz. That's why he can hear dog whistles and you can't.

Vision

Dogs have the advantage when it comes to seeing in dim light. Their greater proportion of rod visual receptors (as compared to cones) allows them to run in the dark without tripping. Dogs are also adept at discerning slight movements, which is why your Aussie is able to read subtle changes in your facial expression and body position. But your Aussie can't see colors like you can. Dogs have color vision like people who are typical red-green color blind; that is, they can tell blue from yellow but confuse reds, oranges, yellows, and greens. Even though dogs do see colors, they don't seem to pay a lot of attention to them. Aussies with bluish white eyes do not appear to have any visual problems compared to Aussies with dark eyes.

Taste

Aussies seem like they'll eat anything! Dogs actually don't taste salt as readily as people do. And while dogs enjoy sweets, they don't like saccharin, probably because it's been shown that their tastebuds respond more to the bitter aftertaste than they do to any sweet aspect.

Touch

Puppies grow up needing to be touched by their dam and littermates, especially when sleeping, and this trait often remains throughout life. Aussies especially enjoy being touched and petted, and yours may shove his head under your hand to remind you of your duties. When adult dogs are petted, their heart and breathing rates decrease, and they appear calmer. The best way to calm a dog through petting is to use deep muscle massage with long, firm strokes reaching from the head to the rear. Petting a dog has also been shown to calm people and lower their blood pressure.

Chapter Six

Health and Nutrition

Your Aussie depends on you to provide the care he needs to live a long and healthy life. This means providing the basic vaccinations and nutrition, along with trips to the veterinarian for annual checkups and occasional injuries or illnesses.

Routine Veterinary Care

With luck, most of your visits to the veterinarian will be for routine care. Nonetheless, you should establish your dog as a patient well ahead of the time you may need a veterinarian for an illness or emergency.

Veterinary Choice

Some breeds require a veterinarian with a lot of experience with that particular breed; fortunately, Aussies have few breed health idiosyncrasies that require much special training. Familiarity with the MDR1 mutation (see page 110) and its implications is probably the most important Aussie-specific knowledge an Australian Shepherd's veterinarian should have.

As far as general requirements, consider availability, emergency arrangements, facilities, costs, ability to communicate, and interaction with your dog. A practice with several veterinarians can often provide more services than one with a single veterinarian, but it may not have the same personal approach. Most veterinarians in general practice can provide a wide range of services, but if your dog has a problem that eludes diagnosis or requires specialized treatment, let your veterinarian know if you are willing to be referred to a specialist. Veterinary specialists can be found at veterinary schools and in private practices in larger cities, but expect to pay much higher fees to see one.

Health Insurance

Even routine dog care can cut into a budget. But what if your dog needs emergency surgery or develops a chronic illness? Even as we welcome the advances in veterinary care that often save our dogs' lives, we also have to acknowledge that cutting-edge procedures may be beyond the budgets of many pet owners.

Pet health insurance can make the difference between life-saving treatment or euthanasia for your dog. Most policies cost from $100 to $500 a year, depending on your dog's age, breed, and where you live. As with human policies, premiums cost more for older dogs; some companies will not insure older dogs at all. With costs for typical accidents and illnesses running in the hundreds to thousands of dollars, such policies can quickly pay for themselves. Fortunately, unlike the typical human health insurance policy, pet policies are usually straightforward and easy to understand. Most have several different plans from which to choose, differing in coverage benefits, length of the policy, and the amount of the required deductible. Most have exclusions for preexisting conditions and, possibly, hereditary defects. It pays to shop around and find the policy that best fits your particular needs. Many policies offer discounts for multiple pets. Most policies allow you to use your own veterinarian, but a few require that you use a veterinarian in their network.

As with all insurance, you are betting that your dog will be sick or injured and need expensive veterinary care. If your dog tends to swallow foreign objects, get into fights, or escape from the yard, or if he has a family history of certain chronic diseases, it's a good bet pet insurance will pay off. If not, you may be better off to take the money you would otherwise spend on premiums and put it in a savings account earmarked for veterinary care.

Breed Truths

DNA Testing

DNA tests can tell you whether or not your Aussie carries genes for certain conditions before he ever develops the condition. Because DNA is constant throughout life, these tests can yield accurate results even in newborn puppies. Most require only swabbing the inside of the cheek with a soft brush and mailing in the sample.

One of the first DNA tests you should have performed on your Aussie is that for the MDR1 mutation. The results of this test will tell you if you have to avoid certain medications at doses that are normally prescribed. See page 110 for more information. The only Aussies that do not need this test are ones whose parents have both tested negative for the mutant gene.

You may consider having another DNA test for cataracts performed. A mutation in the HSF4 gene is associated with a much higher risk of hereditary cataracts. The test is not 100 percent predictive of cataracts because the trait is inherited as an incomplete dominant. However, it is still very informative. See page 96 for more information.

DNA tests are also available for cobalamin malabsorption, a serious disorder in which vitamin B_{12} is not adequately absorbed, and for prcd progressive retinal atrophy, a serious retinal disorder leading to blindness. Both conditions have been reported in Aussies, but they are not common. See pages 97 and 102 for more information.

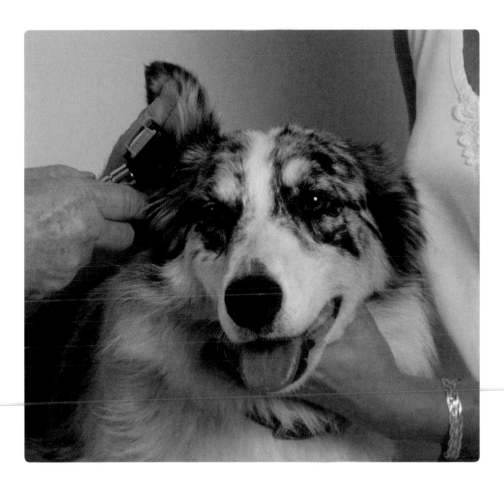

Wellness Exams

Besides going to the veterinarian when he's sick, your Aussie needs an annual wellness examination. Because dogs age faster than humans, a yearly physical in a dog is like a person having one every five years or so, so some veterinarians even advocate twice-yearly exams.

One year after your Aussie's final puppy vaccinations, at around 16 months of age, your Aussie should visit the veterinarian for his adult booster. This is also a good time for his yearly checkup, or wellness examination. A wellness exam typically consists of checking the mouth, teeth, eyes, ears, and genitals; listening to the heart and lungs; feeling along the spine; pressing against the abdomen in order to feel internal organs; and very likely drawing blood for a heartworm test and getting a stool sample to check for intestinal parasites. Some veterinarians also draw a blood sample so that they have baseline values to compare to later samples should your dog ever become sick. If your Aussie is ill, the veterinarian will perform many of these same exams and possibly some specialized tests, depending on the nature of the illness.

Blood Tests

Some of the most common and informative tests your veterinarian may perform are blood tests, which include a complete blood count (CBC) and a serum chemistry profile. The CBC checks red and white blood cells, and can identify problems such as anemia, leukemia, and the presence of many infections. A serum chemistry profile provides information on how various organs are functioning. Within minutes the results can tell you if your dog feels ill because of kidney failure, liver disease, or pancreatitis, for example, enabling the veterinarian to start treatment immediately.

Signs of Sickness

Your veterinarian may use sophisticated tests to detect and diagnose health problems, but you have an even more powerful weapon: the knowledge of what's normal for your dog. Be on the lookout for signs that he's not feeling well.

CAUTION

Diarrhea, Diarrhea Medicine, and the MDR1 Gene

Diarrhea can result from nervousness, a change in diet or water, food sensitivities, intestinal parasites, infections, poisoning, or many other illnesses. It's not uncommon for dogs to have blood in their diarrhea, but diarrhea with lots of blood, or accompanied by vomiting, fever, or other symptoms of illness, warrants a call to the veterinarian. Bright red blood indicates a source lower in the digestive tract, while dark black, tarry stools indicate a source higher in the digestive tract. In most adult Aussie cases, the best treatment is to withhold food for 24 hours, and then feed rice and low-fat foods. Ask your veterinarian about using antidiarrhea medication. **Warning:** Loperamide, an antidiarrheal agent found in many popular human diarrhea medicines, is not safe even at normal doses for Aussies with the mutant MDR1 gene. For more information about the gene, see page 110.

Lethargy

Lethargy is the most common sign of illness. Possible causes include:

- Infection (check for fever)
- Anemia (check gum color)
- Circulatory problem (check pulse and gum color)
- Pain (check limbs, neck, back, mouth, eyes, ears, and abdomen for signs)
- Nausea
- Poisoning (check gum color and pupil reaction; look for vomiting or abdominal pain)
- Sudden vision loss
- Cancer
- Metabolic diseases

FYI: Changes in Appearance or Behavior

These signs	may indicate (among other causes)
Restlessness, retching, bowing	gut obstruction—EMERGENCY
Inability to urinate	blockage—EMERGENCY
Enlarged abdomen, sudden bloat	internal bleeding—EMERGENCY
Lying in a curled position	fever, general illness, weakness
Irritability, restlessness	pain
Clawing, panting, trembling, hiding	pain, fear
Repeated stretching and bowing	abdominal pain
Pain when head is lifted	neck pain, disc disease
Refusal to lie down	breathing problems, abdominal pain
Refusal to put head down	breathing problems, neck pain
Head-pressing, seizures	neurological problems
Weakness, pale gums	illness, internal bleeding, anemia
Dizziness, head tilt	vestibular disease, ear infection
Loss of appetite	illness, fever, kidney disease
Increased appetite	Cushing's, diabetes
Increased thirst (and urination)	diabetes, kidney disease, Cushing's
Frequent, sudden, painful urination	urinary tract infection
Difficult, painful urination; bloody urine	kidney or bladder stones
Regurgitating food right after eating	esophageal/swallowing problem
Vomiting	illness, poisoning, blockage
Coughing	kennel cough, heart disease, tracheal collapse
Gagging (chronic)	tracheal collapse, laryngeal paralysis, foreign body
Enlarged abdomen, progressive	Cushing's, pregnancy, pyometra, heart failure

Note that many other problems can cause these signs. You should always consult your veterinarian as soon as possible for a diagnosis and treatment.

FYI: Gum Color

Your Aussie's gum color is the window to his blood and should be one of the first things you check when you suspect illness. Gums should be a deep pink, and if you press on them with your thumb, they should return to pink within two seconds after lifting your thumb (a longer time suggests a circulatory problem).

Gum color	could mean
Pale or white	anemia, shock, internal bleeding
Bluish	lack of oxygen, poor circulation
Bright red	overheating, carbon monoxide poisoning
Brick red	high fever
Yellowish	liver disease
Red splotches	blood clotting problem

Temperature

To take your Aussie's temperature, lubricate a plastic (never glass) digital rectal thermometer and insert it about 2 inches (5 centimeters) into the dog's anus, leaving it there for about a minute. Normal is 101–102°F (38.3–38.9°C). If the temperature is

- 103°F (39.4°C) or above, call your veterinarian. This is not usually an emergency but is a concern.
- 104°F (40°C) or above, go to your veterinarian.
- 105°F or above, this is an emergency. Try to cool your dog by dampening his fur and placing him in front of a fan. Do not dunk him in icy water, which constricts surface vessels and traps the heat at the body core. Stop cooling him when the temperature is down to 103°F. Take him to the veterinarian.
- 98°F (36.6°C) or below, call your veterinarian. Try to warm your dog.
- 97°F (36.1°C) or below, go to your veterinarian. Treat for hypothermia on the way by warming your dog with hot water bottles or blankets.

Pulse

When at rest, an adult Aussie's pulse should be fewer than 25 beats per minute. Feel the pulse on his chest or inner thigh. Puppy pulses are higher; if the pulse is reliably over 25, consult your veterinarian.

CHECKLIST

The Home Checkup

Make several copies of this checklist and keep a record of your dog's home checkups. Check the following:

Weight: _____

☐ Increased? ☐ Decreased?

Mouth: ☐ Loose teeth? ☐ Painful? ☐ Dirty? ☐ Bad breath?

Gums: ☐ Swellings? ☐ Bleeding? ☐ Sores? ☐ Growths?

Gum color: ☐ Pink (good)? ☐ Bright red? ☐ Bluish?
☐ Whitish? ☐ Red spots?

Nose: ☐ Thick or colored discharge? ☐ Cracking?
☐ Pinched? ☐ Sores?

Eyes: ☐ Tearing? ☐ Mucous discharge? ☐ Dull surface?
☐ Squinting? ☐ Swelling? ☐ Redness?
☐ Unequal pupils? ☐ Pawing at eyes?

Ears: ☐ Bad smell? ☐ Redness? ☐ Abundant debris?
☐ Scabby ear tips? ☐ Head shaking? ☐ Head tilt?
☐ Ear scratching? ☐ Painfulness?

Legs: ☐ Asymmetrical bones or muscles? ☐ Lumps?
☐ Weakness? ☐ Limping?

Feet: ☐ Long or split nails? ☐ Cut pads?
☐ Swollen or misaligned toes?

Skin: ☐ Parasites? ☐ Black grains (flea dirt)? ☐ Hair loss? ☐ Scabs?
☐ Greasy patches? ☐ Bad odor? ☐ Lumps?

Abdomen: ☐ Bloated? ☐ Pendulous? ☐ Painful?

Anal and genital regions:

☐ Swelling? ☐ Discharge? ☐ Redness?
☐ Bloody urine? ☐ Bloody or blackened diarrhea?
☐ Worms in stool or around anus?
☐ Scooting rear? ☐ Licking rear?

If you answered yes to anything abnormal on the checklist, contact your veterinarian for advice.

Hereditary Disorders

Every breed of dog has its own set of hereditary headaches when it comes to health problems. In some cases one or more of the breed's founding dogs happened to have the genes for that problem, and because of the closed gene pool that makes up a breed, those genes became widespread. A good example of this in Aussies is the MDR1 mutation (see page 110), which actually arose in ancestors of the Aussie before it was even a breed. In other cases the problem is a secondary effect of some aspect of the dog's desired conformation. Because the Aussie is a dog of moderate conformation, it has few such conditions. One of them might be an iris coloboma, which is seen almost exclusively in merles.

Fortunately, the Aussie is not overwhelmed with hereditary problems, although it does have several problems to which it is more prone compared with other breeds. Surveys taken by the Australian Shepherd Health & Genetics Institute (ASHGI) provide information about health problems that have been reported in Aussies. You can learn more about Aussie health and partake in the health surveys by going to the institute's website at *www.ashgi.org.*

Note that simply because a condition is considered "more frequent" doesn't mean it's rampant in the breed. If, for example, one out of fifty Aussies has a particular condition, that's common enough to be considered "more frequent" but certainly not so common that the next Aussie you see will have it. It does, however, mean that breeders should be aware of these potential problems, test for them when possible, and avoid breeding dogs with a background of similar problems together. According to ASHGI, the following hereditary problems are seen in Aussies:

More frequent

- Cataracts: opacities in the eye's lens at a young age
- Epilepsy: repeated seizures of unknown cause
- Dental faults: under- and overbites, as well as missing teeth
- Autoimmune disease: the immune system turning on part of the dog's own body
- Hip dysplasia: improperly formed hip joint resulting in joint laxity and lameness
- Iris coloboma: missing area of the eye's iris
- Allergies: inhalation, flea, or food allergies, mostly resulting in itchy skin
- Cancer (not all hereditary): hemangiosarcoma and lymphosarcoma most frequent
- Distichiasis: extra lashes that grow toward the eye's cornea
- Cryptorchidism: one or both testicles failing to descend into the scrotum
- Collie eye anomaly: patches of underdeveloped choroid layer of the eye
- Elbow dysplasia: malformation of the elbow joint, causing lameness

Less frequent (but still seen enough to be of concern)

- Persistent pupillary membrane: tendrils of membrane extending across the eye's pupil
- Corneal dystrophy: opacities on the eye's cornea
- Hemophilia A and B: blood clotting disorder leading to excessive bleeding
- Muscular dystrophy: muscle disorder leading to weakness
- Osteochondritis dissecans: painful joint disorder mostly seen in elbow or shoulder joints
- Patellar luxation: slipped kneecaps
- Patent ductus arteriosus: heart defect
- Pelger-Huet anomaly: killer of unborn and newborn puppies; carriers are healthy
- Cobalamin malabsorption: reduced ability to absorb vitamin B_{12}
- Progressive retinal atrophy: eye disease leading to blindness
- Rage syndrome: sudden unpredictable aggressive outbursts
- von Willebrand's disease: blood clotting disorder leading to excessive bleeding

Hereditary Eye Problems

As in many breeds, several of the more common hereditary problems in Aussie's involve the eyes. Hereditary cataracts are the most frequently seen problem. Aussies should have their eyes checked yearly, and breeding stock should have a CERF (Canine Eye Registration Foundation), *www.vmdb.org/cerf.html*, examination and clearance within a year of being bred and up to 9 years of age once retired from breeding.

Cataracts, or opaque areas in the lenses, are the most common hereditary eye problem in Aussies. They most often appear between 2 and 3 years of age, although some appear as late as 8 years. A cataract in one eye is usually followed by one in the other eye within the year. Not all cataracts are hereditary; some can come with age or as a result of trauma. The bluish tinge you see in an older dog's lenses is normal aging and should not be confused with cataracts. Cataracts become whitish and opaque, interfering with vision. An ophthalmologist can remove the affected lenses and replace them with an artificial lens. If they are removed but not replaced, your Aussie will be able to see shapes but will not be able to bring them into focus. A DNA test is available from the Animal Health Trust in Britain (*www.aht.org.uk/genetics_tests.html*). The mode of inheritance is dominant with incomplete penetrance, meaning that dogs with the mutation will develop the condition to various degrees, and some not at all. Dogs with one copy of the mutant gene are significantly more likely to develop cataracts than dogs with no copies of it; dogs with two copies of the mutant gene are more likely to have more severe cataracts.

Iris colobomas, in which a piece of the iris is missing, are the second most common hereditary eye problem in the breed. They occur almost exclusively in merles, and usually affect just one eye. If large enough, a coloboma can cause discomfort in bright light, but most colobomas are small and don't affect vision.

Persistent pupillary membranes (PPM) are thin strings of membrane that extend from one edge of the iris margin that surrounds the pupil. They sometimes disappear as a puppy ages, but those that remain at 6 months of age will probably remain for life. Those that extend from one side of the iris to the other seldom affect vision, but those that extend from the iris to attach to the cornea or lens can lead to blindness. Fortunately, the latter type is rare in Aussies.

Distichiasis refers to extra or abnormal eyelashes that grow toward the eye, possibly irritating the cornea. If they do rub on the cornea, they must be surgically removed so that the cornea is not scarred and the dog is not in pain. The mode of inheritance is not known.

Collie eye anomaly (CEA) is a hereditary eye disorder in which the choroid layer of the eye, which is responsible for blood circulation in the eye, is underdeveloped at birth and remains so. Dogs with mild cases will never exhibit any noticeable signs. In severe cases, which make up about 25 percent of affected dogs, partial blindness can result from retinal detachment in areas in which the choroid is especially thin. CEA is inherited as a recessive trait. The same gene is responsible for both mild and severe cases. Your veterinarian can detect the problem most easily at 5 to 8 weeks of age by looking into your dog's eye with an ophthalmoscope. After that age it

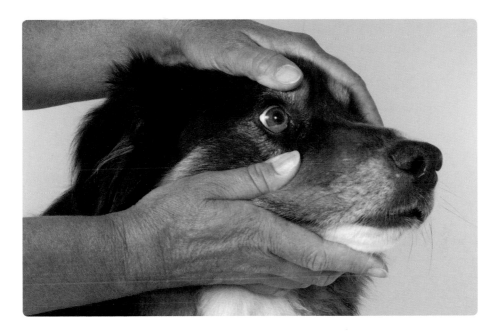

may be harder to detect, as the trait becomes masked in some eyes. Breeders used to say that such eyes would "go normal," but they do not return to normal; the trait is simply obscured. These dogs still have two recessive genes for CEA and can pass them on. A DNA test available from OptiGen (*www.optigen.com*) can detect the presence of the gene that causes CEA, but the test cannot determine its severity. The frequency of CEA in Aussies has decreased over the last few decades.

Corneal dystrophy, in which an opaque area occurs on the corneal surface, can range from mild to blinding. The condition may be hereditary or may be secondary to thyroid disease. The first signs are whitish opacities on the cornea. They can be round, oval, or ring-shaped and usually occur in both eyes. Mild cases can go untreated, but eye drops may prevent them from getting worse. Advanced cases may need antibiotic eye drops as well as surgery.

Merle ocular dysgenesis occurs only in double-merle (homozygous merle) Aussies. The condition may include abnormally small eyes (micro-phthalmia), non-centered pupils, colobomas, cataracts, PPM, lens luxation (detached lens), and retinal dysplasia. Many affected dogs are blind. The condition can be avoided by never breeding merle to merle.

Progressive retinal atrophy (PRA), has been reported in Aussies but is rare. PRA comes in several forms; the form that Aussies have is progressive rod-cone degeneration (prcd), which is the most widespread form of PRA among all breeds. It is inherited as a recessive trait; dogs with one copy of the gene have no problems, but those with two copies gradually lose their sight starting in middle age. A DNA test is available through OptiGen (*www.optigen.com*).

Hereditary Health Testing Regime Suggested by the Australian Shepherd Health & Genetics Institute

Recommended Age	Test	Performed By	Breeding Status: Two copies of mutation
5–8 weeks	Eye exam	Veterinary ophthalmologist	CEA: DNB Iris coloboma: DNB Ditichiasis & PPM: See Comments
	Heart check	Small animal veterinarian	Congenital defects: DNB
4 mos	Heart recheck	Small animal veterinarian	Congenital defects: DNB
	Hernia exam	Breeder or small animal veterinarian	See Comments
6 mos	MDR1	Testing lab	Breed only to clear
	Cataract DNA test	Testing lab	DNB
	CEA	Testing lab	DNB
	Cobalamine malabsorption	Testing lab	DNB
	PHA	Small animal veterinarian or pathology lab	N/A
	Cardiac	Veterinary cardiologist	DNB
	Hemophilia/ von Willebrand's	Testing lab	DNB
	PRA	Testing lab	DNB
12 months	Eye exam	Veterinary ophthalmologist	Cataracts: DNB Iris coloboma: DNB Ditichiasis & PPM: See Comments
	Patellas	Small animal veterinarian	DNB
	Thyroid	Qualified lab	DNB
2 years	Hips	Small animal veterinarian	DNB
	Elbows	Small animal veterinarian	DNB
	Eye exam	Veterinary ophthalmologist	Cataracts: DNB All others: As above.
3–9 years	Eye exam	Veterinary ophthalmologist	Cataracts: DNB All others: As above.

DNB = Do Not Breed
Reprinted with Permission from the Australian Shepherd Health & Genetics Institute

Breeding Status: One copy of mutation	Comments
N/A	ALL Aussie puppies should have an eye exam. Puppies with PPM should be rechecked at 6–12 months. Puppies with multiple distichia or distichia causing corneal abrasions should not be bred.
N/A	Test puppies with family history of patent ductus arteriosis or other congenital heart defects. Puppies with congenital heart defects should not be bred. Recheck if necessary.
N/A	Upon advice of veterinarian.
N/A	If surgical correction is required, do not breed. All others, do not breed to affecteds or their close kin.
Breed only to clear	Testing should be done before dog receives any MDR1-sensitive drugs. Any dog with the mutation should not receive MDR1-sensitive drugs.
Dominant: DNB	Even one copy of this mutation causes extremely high risk for cataracts.
Breed only to clear	Test all dogs with a family history.
Breed only to clear	Test all dogs with a family history.
Breed only to clear	Lethal to fetuses and neonates. Test all dogs with a family history.
N/A	If there is a family history of congenital heart defects.
N/A	Necessary only if dog shows evidence of clotting disorder.
Breed only to clear	Test all dogs with family history.
N/A	Dogs with lens or cornea PPM attachments should not be bred. Dogs with multiple distichia or distichia causing corneal abrasions should not be bred.
N/A	Test all dogs with a family history.
N/A	Use OFA-approved panel.
N/A	Exam age may vary depending on screening program used.
N/A	Exam age may vary depending on screening program used.
N/A	
N/A	

Other Hereditary Problems

Although eye problems combined make up one of the largest concerns in terms of frequency, other hereditary problems are of greater concern because of their effect on quality of life or life span.

Epilepsy, the breed's most common serious hereditary health problem, is a brain disorder characterized by repeated seizures with no apparent structural brain abnormality. Epilepsy must be differentiated from other brain or physiological disorders that cause seizures. Reports of Aussies with epilepsy seem to be on the rise, with the condition typically appearing between 1.5 to 3 years of age. Seizure activity is most common when the dog is resting, often in the early morning or nighttime. Seizures range from mild, with no loss of consciousness and only subtle incoordination and mental abnormalities, to severe grand mal seizures with full convulsions. Severe seizures are characterized by a stiff body, chomping of the jaws, extreme salivation, loss of bladder and bowel control, vocalization, paddling, or any combination of these signs. After a seizure, the dog will experience a period of confusion and disorientation, often including pacing and apparent blindness. It may take minutes or hours for full recovery. The seizures may be infrequent at first but become more frequent and severe over time, especially if untreated. Medication can help many dogs live normal lives; however, not all dogs respond adequately, and some must be euthanized if the seizures become overwhelmingly frequent and incapacitating. The condition appears to have a hereditary basis, so affected dogs should not be bred.

Hip dysplasia, in which the hip joint is not properly formed, can result in crippling lameness. Dogs with hip dysplasia may have episodes of lameness of the rear legs that worsen with exercise, or they may have difficulty rising, walking, climbing stairs, and running. Later, they may develop arthritis and consistent lameness, and they may shift their weight forward when standing. Diagnosing hip dysplasia requires radiographs (X rays) of the dog's hips, usually under sedation. Breeding stock should be screened either through the Orthopedic Foundation for Animals (OFA; *www.offa.org*) or the University of Pennsylvania Hip Improvement Program (PennHIP; *www.pennhip.org*). Once hip dysplasia is diagnosed, the treatment options vary from conservative medical care to more aggressive surgical care to total hip replacement. Hip dysplasia is inherited in a polygenic manner, meaning it results from the interplay of several as-yet-unidentified genes. About 6 percent of Aussies registered with the OFA are dysplastic, although the Australian Shepherd Club of America DNA committee survey found that about 20 percent of Aussies in the survey sample were dysplastic.

Elbow dysplasia encompasses several problems, all of which eventually lead to degenerative joint disease of the elbow. Symptoms, which can appear in dogs as young as 4 months of age, include varying degrees of swelling, pain, and lameness originating in the elbow joint. Radiographs (X rays) are the usual way to diagnose the condition, but they may not detect every case, especially in very young dogs. Treatment is with surgery, which can be expensive. Left untreated, the condition becomes progressively more painful. The OFA maintains an elbow registry for dogs over 2 years of age. Abnormal elbows are assigned either Grade I, II, or III, with Grade III being the most severely affected. About 4 percent of Aussies in the OFA database are reported to have elbow dysplasia, with most of them rated Grade I. Because of the crippling nature of this disorder, affected dogs should not be bred.

Hemangiosarcoma is a malignant cancer that affects the lining of the blood vessels. It is most often found in the spleen, heart, or liver but can also arise in the bone or skin. It is the most common type of cancer reported in Aussies, and it is usually fatal. It is not only common in Aussies, however; many breeds, especially large breeds, are affected by this cancer. Very often the first sign is sudden weakness or collapse, with extremely pale gums. This occurs because the tumor bleeds, and the internal bleeding leads to hypovolemic shock. If the bleeding does not stop, death can occur within hours, even minutes. If the bleeding is from a tumor of the spleen or liver, the abdomen may be enlarged and filled with fluid. In most cases, except for hemangiosarcoma of the skin, the tumor has already been carried throughout the body by the bloodstream by the time it's diagnosed.

Lymphoma is the second most commonly seen cancer in Aussies. Also called lymphosarcoma, lymphoma affects the lymphocytes, which are cells that normally function as part of the immune system. Because lymphoma can affect many parts of the body, no one set of signs defines it. Many forms are first noticed when the dog becomes lethargic and loses weight and appetite. Some dogs may have one or more enlarged lymph nodes. If abdominal organs are involved, the abdomen may be distended, and the dog may vomit. Other forms may cause coughing, drooling, and difficulty swallowing. Lymphoma

CAUTION

Medications

Never give human medications to your dog unless your veterinarian tells you to do so. Some human medications work on dogs but must be used at different strengths, and some have no effect or bad effects on dogs. Always give the full course of medications prescribed by your veterinarian, even if your dog appears well. Otherwise the problem can return and be more resistant to the medication next time.

Remember that Aussies with the MDR1 mutation cannot safely ingest many of the same medications that are safe for other dogs. This includes some human medications, such as loperamide for diarrhea, that are commonly suggested for dogs.

To give a pill, open your dog's mouth and place the pill well in the rear of the mouth. Close the mouth and gently stroke the throat until he swallows. Or just hide the pill in some liverwurst or other soft treat and watch to make sure he eats it. To give liquid medication, place the liquid in the side of the mouth and let the dog swallow. Don't squirt it in so that the dog inhales it.

is one of the most responsive cancers to chemotherapy, although success is variable and relapses usually occur. Dogs undergoing chemotherapy usually have a good quality of life and do not suffer the side effects that people do.

Cobalamin malabsorption is a potentially life-threatening recessively inherited disorder in which vitamin B_{12} is not adequately absorbed. Signs, which include lethargy, lack of appetite, general ill health, wasting, vomiting, and seizures, may begin as early as 6 weeks of age but may not be obvious enough to notice until adulthood. Special diagnostic tests and a DNA test are available; for more information go to the ASHGI website. Treatment is lifelong vitamin B_{12} injections every two to four weeks.

Misdiagnoses Sometimes Aussies are misdiagnosed with common disorders when in fact they have a hereditary disorder that is rare in other breeds. Cobalamin malabsorption is one such example, as it is sometimes confused with a liver shunt. If your Aussie is not responding as he should be to a treatment for a disorder, consult the ASHGI website for "imitators" that might be masquerading as another disease.

Emergencies

First aid doesn't take the place of veterinary attention. In every case below, first call the veterinarian and then apply first aid as you're transporting the dog. Move the dog as little as possible to get him to a safe place. Be ready to treat for shock.

Shock Signs of shock are weakness, collapse, pale gums, unresponsiveness, and faint pulse. Since it may occur in almost any case of trauma, it's usually best to treat the dog as though he were in shock. Keep him warm and quiet, and keep his head low compared to his heart (unless he has a head wound).

Heatstroke Early signs of heatstroke include rapid loud breathing, abundant thick saliva, bright red mucous membranes, and high rectal temperature. Later signs include unsteadiness, diarrhea, and coma.

Wet the dog down and place him in front of a fan. If this isn't possible immerse him in cold water. Don't plunge him in ice water, because that constricts the peripheral blood vessels so much that they can't cool the blood as well. Offer water to drink. You must lower your dog's body temperature

Helpful Hints

The First Aid Kit

- Emergency veterinary phone number
- First aid instructions
- Rectal thermometer
- Scissors
- Hemostats
- Sterile gauze dressings
- Self-adhesive bandage
- Antiseptic skin ointment
- Instant cold compress
- Antidiarrheal medication
- Allergy medication
- Ophthalmic ointment
- Pen light
- Hydrogen peroxide
- Activated charcoal
- Tongue depressor
- Soap

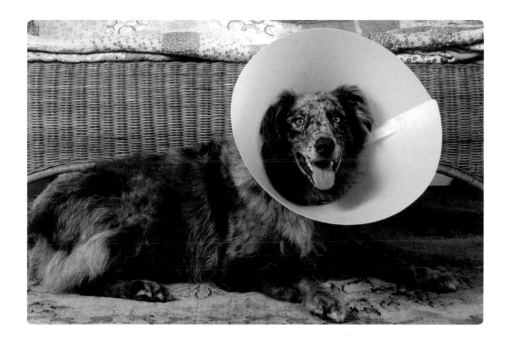

quickly, but don't let the temperature go below 100°F. Stop cooling when the rectal temperature reaches 103°F, as it will continue to fall.

Even when the temperature is back to normal, your Aussie is still in danger and needs veterinary attention. It will take several days for your dog to recover, during which time he should not exert himself.

Bleeding To control bleeding, cover the wound with a clean dressing and apply pressure. Apply more dressings over any blood-soaked ones until the bleeding stops. Elevating the wound site and applying a cold pack to the area will also slow bleeding. If the wound is on a front leg, apply pressure to the inside of the front leg just above the elbow. If it's on a rear leg, apply pressure inside the thigh where the femoral artery crosses the thigh bone.

Stings Insect stings can sometimes cause allergic reactions. Swelling around the nose and throat can block the airways. Other possible reactions include restlessness, vomiting, diarrhea, seizures, and collapse. At the slightest hint of a reaction give an allergy pill (ask your veterinarian for the best type to keep in your first aid kit and how much to give).

Seizures A dog having a seizure may drool, stiffen, yelp, or twitch uncontrollably. Wrap the dog in a blanket and keep him away from stairs and other dogs. Never put your hands or anything in a convulsing dog's mouth. Make note of everything you can remember about the seizure, which may help determine the cause.

Poisoning Signs of poisoning vary according to the type of poison but often include vomiting, depression, and convulsions. When in doubt call your veterinarian or an animal poison control hotline. If the poison was ingested in the past two hours, and if it's not an acid, alkali, petroleum product, solvent, or tranquilizer, you may be advised to induce vomiting by giving hydrogen peroxide or dry mustard mixed in equal parts with water. Ipecac syrup is not recommended for this purpose in dogs. In other cases you may be advised to dilute the poison by giving milk or vegetable oil. Activated charcoal can absorb many toxins. Poisons act in different ways, so it's important to have the label of any suspected poisons available.

- Ethylene glycol-based antifreeze is a dog killer. Even tiny amounts can cause irreversible kidney damage, and the prognosis is poor once symptoms appear. Get emergency help if you suspect your dog drank antifreeze.
- Rodent poisons are either warfarin-based, which can cause uncontrolled internal bleeding, or cholecalciferol-based, which can cause kidney failure.
- Bird and squirrel poisons are usually strychnine-based, which can cause neurological malfunction.
- Insect poisons, weed killers, and wood preservatives may be arsenic-based, which can cause kidney failure.
- Flea, tick, and internal parasite poisons may contain organophosphates, which can cause neurological symptoms.
- Iron-based rose fertilizers can cause kidney and liver failure.

Australian Shepherd Nutrition

Choosing your Aussie's diet can be confusing. There are no hard and fast rules that apply to every dog, so you have to make a decision based on what fits your time and budget, what makes your Aussie look and act healthy, and what your Aussie enjoys eating. The last part is pretty easy; most Aussies are not exactly discriminating when it comes to food!

Commercial or Home-Prepared Diet?

Many people seek alternatives to commercial foods in belief that they are not a natural way to feed dogs and that dogs do better when fed fresh, whole foods with top-quality ingredients. Although these points are true, it can be difficult to design a balanced diet on your own. If homemade diets are prepared according to recipes devised by certified canine nutritionists, they should have the correct proportion of nutrients. One caveat is that, unlike commercial dog foods, such diets are not customarily tested on generations of dogs, which makes them vulnerable to looking healthy on paper but not being properly digested or utilized. They can also be labor intensive, although large batches can be made and frozen.

Some people prefer to feed their dogs a BARF (Bones and Raw Food) diet, consisting of raw meaty bones along with vegetables, with the idea that such a diet better emulates that of a wild dog. Although dogs have better resistance to bacterial food poisoning than do humans, BARF diets have

BE PREPARED! Dangerous Table Scraps

A few table scraps won't hurt, as long as they don't cut into your Aussie's balanced diet. But choose your scraps carefully. Avoid hunks of fat, which can bring on pancreatitis in susceptible dogs, and avoid the following human foods that are toxic to dogs.

- Chocolate contains the stimulant theobromine, which can cause shaking, seizures, increased heart rate, and death in dogs. Milk chocolate has about 44 milligrams of theobromine per ounce, semisweet chocolate about 150 milligrams per ounce, and baker's chocolate about 390 milligrams per ounce. About 50 to 100 milligrams per pound is considered a lethal dose for dogs.
- Coffee in high amounts, and especially coffee beans or grounds, can cause caffeine toxicity in dogs.
- Sugar-free candy and gum containing the artificial sweetener xylitol can cause a potentially fatal drop in blood sugar and lead to liver failure.
- Onions cause a condition in which the red blood cells are destroyed, in extreme cases leading to anemia and even death. Garlic contains the same ingredient but in lesser quantity.
- Macadamia nuts cause some dogs to become very ill; the cause isn't understood.
- Raisins and grapes can cause kidney failure and extreme sudden toxicity in some dogs. As little as 0.3 ounces of grapes per pound and 0.05 ounces of raisins per pound have caused kidney failure in some dogs.
- Yeast bread dough can rise in the gastrointestinal tract, causing obstruction. It also produces alcohol as it rises.
- Alcohol can make dogs drunk just as it does people. It can also kill dogs if they drink too much.
- Raw eggs, contrary to popular opinion, are not good for dogs. They prevent the absorption of biotin, an important B vitamin. They can also contain salmonella.
- Apple, apricot, cherry, peach, and plum pits and stems contain a cyanide-type compound. Signs of toxicity include dilated pupils, difficulty breathing, fast breathing, and shock.
- Nutmeg in large amounts can cause toxicity in dogs. Signs include tremors, seizures, and even death.
- Spoiled food is no safer for dogs than it is for you. It can cause food poisoning, with signs including vomiting, diarrhea, and even death. Moldy food can cause nervous system signs such as tremors.

occasionally been associated with food poisoning, often from salmonella, in dogs. Commercially available meats may be awash in contaminated liquids. Veterinary nutritionists advise that if you do feed raw meat, do not feed ground meat, and sear the meat to kill bacteria on the surface, which is where most pathogens are found.

Advocates of home-prepared diets claim their dogs have cleaner teeth, fresher breath, better skin, increased vigor, and decreased incidence of bloat. Detractors warn of tooth fractures, intestinal perforations and impactions, pancreatitis, eclampsia, fever, and toxemia. A 2001 study analyzed the nutritional content of two commercial raw diets and three homemade raw diets made to recipe specifications, and found that the homemade diets, especially, had various nutrient deficiencies and vitamin and mineral excesses. They had particularly high vitamin D and were deficient in sodium and phosphorus, with abnormal calcium-to-phosphorus ratios that can lead to hyperparathyroidism. No controlled studies have been performed to compare health and longevity in dogs fed home-prepared or raw diets to those fed commercial-prepared diets. No doubt long-lived dogs have thrived on both types, just as humans manage to thrive on a variety of diets.

Commercial Dog Food

Comparing commercial dog foods can be confusing, but a good place to start is understanding dog food labels. Words such as "stew" or in "gel," "aspic," or "gravy" indicate the food contains more moisture, and while that moisture tends to make the food tastier, it also means you're paying more for what you get. The words "dinner" and "entrée" mean the food must be 25 to 95 percent of the specified meat, whereas the words "with" or "and" mean the food contains 3 to 25 percent of the specified meat.

All ingredients in a food must be listed in order according to percentage weight, from highest to lowest. It's generally a good rule of thumb to look for foods in which the first several ingredients are mostly meat-based. Unfortunately, the ingredient list can be misleading. For example, by breaking down a less desirable ingredient into different forms, which are then listed separately, the predominant ingredient may instead look like several less important ingredients. A food with the ingredients "chicken, wheat germ meal, wheat middlings, wheat bran, wheat flour," for instance, probably has wheat, not chicken, as its primary ingredient. In addition, some ingredients, such as fresh meat, weigh more simply because of their moisture content and may thus be placed higher in the ingredient list of a dry food than their dry matter justifies. Regardless, stick with your rule of thumb: The more meat higher up in the ingredient list, the better.

The guaranteed analysis chart on the food packaging represents the minimum percentages of crude protein and crude fat, and the maximum percentages of crude fiber and moisture that a food contains. Protein represents the building blocks of life, so in general, the more the better. Unfortunately, some proteins are more digestible or have more needed amino acids than others, and the guaranteed analysis doesn't distinguish between them. Fat percentage is handy in comparing the calories a food may contain, as fat has roughly double the calories of protein or carbohydrates. If fiber and moisture content are the same, a higher-fat food will have more calories. Crude fiber is an estimate of how much of the food is indigestible. Higher levels are often found in weight-reducing diets.

You'll notice that dry foods seem packed with nutrition compared to wet foods. That's because wet foods contain so much water it makes their nutritional content look low. Here's a quick way to compare wet and dry food: Multiply the canned values by 4. If the food is "in gravy," multiply them by 5.

Supplements

Most supplements are not necessary when feeding a balanced diet, but a few can be beneficial in some cases of illness.

Essential fatty acids (EFAs) are important in maintaining healthy skin and hair, as well as in kidney function and reproduction. Linoleic acid is found in most vegetable oils and is popular among owners seeking to improve skin and fur quality, especially in cases of itching or disorders producing dry, flaky skin. Omega-3 fatty acids help reduce inflammation and may be helpful for dogs with arthritis, allergies, kidney disease, and heart disease. Omega-6 fatty acids may help synthesize the natural oils of the skin. A little goes a long way; too much of any fatty acid can cause diarrhea or even weight gain.

Chondroitin sulfate and glucosamine are popular supplements for dogs with arthritis, working by affecting the cartilage matrix and synovial membrane. They have been shown to reduce some arthritic symptoms in humans, and studies in dogs show that a combination of the two reduces arthritic signs from cruciate disease.

Coenzyme Q10 (CoQ10) is an antioxidant required for energy production by cells. It's often used for patients with heart disease, allergies, periodontal disease, and sometimes cancer.

Zinc has received a lot of attention in recent years because of its association with healthy skin. Dogs with inadequate levels of zinc in their diets often have hair loss and thickened and scabby skin. Some skin problems are actually termed "zinc-responsive," because they improve with zinc supplementation. Essential fatty acids can increase the body's ability to absorb zinc, whereas excessive calcium supplementation may reduce the absorption of zinc.

Brewer's yeast has long been a popular supplement because of the widespread belief that it helps control fleas. Controlled studies have disputed this claim, but many owners still maintain it works. Because it contains high levels of phosphorus, it shouldn't be used in young puppies or in dogs with kidney problems.

Vitamins and minerals Most commercial diets contain sufficient vitamins and minerals, and it is not necessary to add any. Nonetheless, many owners opt to add a dog vitamin to the daily treats. Vitamins marketed for humans are made for human weight and contain too high a vitamin concentration for smaller dogs unless only a portion is given. Excessive amounts of most vitamins are simply excreted and do no harm, but excessive amounts of some, such as vitamins A and D, can be harmful.

- Excess vitamin A has toxic effects on the liver, especially if the liver is already taxed because of other toxins or drugs.
- Excess vitamin D can lead to kidney damage and cause calcification of soft tissue.

The same is true with minerals. Excessive amounts of most minerals won't harm a normal, healthy dog, but excessive levels can harm dogs with special needs.

- Excess copper can cause liver damage in dogs that cannot excrete copper normally.
- Excess phosphorus in dogs with kidney disease can cause problems similar to those of excessive vitamin D.

- Excess calcium is not appropriate for growing or pregnant dogs. Puppies under 6 months of age are especially susceptible to damage from excess calcium, which can lead to skeletal problems and osteochondrosis. Pregnant bitches given calcium supplements are more prone to develop eclampsia when nursing.

Aussie Weight and Diet

Despite their high activity level, Aussies tend to put on weight easily. In fact, some research indicates that, in general, herding breeds have lower metabolisms than many other dogs, meaning they can maintain weight on relatively low quantities of food.

Gauge how much to feed your Aussie by how much he eats and how much he weighs. You should be able to feel the ribs slightly when you run your hands along the ribcage. An indication of a waistline should be visible both from above and from the side. There should be no fat roll on the withers, and the ribcage should not be rounded out with fat, nor should the front legs be bowed out at the elbows from a fat body.

Some disorders, such as heart disease, Cushing's disease, hypothyroidism, and the early stages of diabetes, can cause a dog to appear fat or pot-bellied. A dog whose abdomen only is enlarged is especially suspect and should be examined by a veterinarian. A bloated belly in a puppy may signal internal parasites.

Most fat-looking Aussies are fat because they simply eat more calories than they burn. They need to lose weight, which you can achieve by feeding smaller portions of a lower-caloric food. Commercially available diet foods supply about 15 percent fewer calories compared to standard foods. Protein levels should remain moderate to high to avoid muscle loss when dieting. It's hard to resist those pleading eyes when your Aussie begs for a treat, but treats add up to lots of calories during the day. Substitute carrot sticks or rice cakes for fattening treats. Keep him away from where you prepare or eat human meals, and instead of feeding him leftovers when you're through eating, make it a habit to go for a walk.

Dog food labels don't include calories, so you may need to calculate them yourself. Proteins and carbohydrates both have about 3.5 calories per gram, and fat has about 8.5 calories per gram. By multiplying 3.5 times the percentage of protein and carbohydrates listed in the analysis, and 8.5 times the percentage of fat, and then adding these products together, you will have the food's total number of calories per gram.

Although thin Aussies are rare compared to fat ones, they do exist, especially when young. A thin adult should be checked by your veterinarian. Unexplained weight loss can be caused by heart disease, cancer, and any number of endocrine problems. If he checks out normal, you may be able to add pounds by feeding more meals of a higher-calorie food. Add canned food, ground beef, or a small amount of chicken fat. Heating the food will often increase its appeal. Or try adding a late-night snack; many dogs seem to have their best appetites late at night.

10 **Questions** About Aussies, Medications, and the MDR1 Gene

1 **Is it true that certain kinds of heartworm preventive can be deadly to Collie-type dogs?**

In 1983 researchers noted a peculiar reaction in some Collies to ivermectin, a drug used for heartworm prevention. These Collies had neurological signs (drooling, stumbling, blindness, coma, respiratory problems, and even death) at doses that were 1/200th of the dose needed to cause problems in other dogs. Some Australian Shepherds had similar symptoms.

2 **What causes the problem?**

The problem can be traced to a mutation in the multi-drug resistance (MDR1) gene, which is needed to form a type of protein that's vital to flushing drugs out of the brain. When this protein is faulty, some drugs, such as ivermectin, remain in the brain, where they build up and cause toxic effects.

3 **Do all Aussies have this gene mutation?**

About 32 percent of Australian Shepherds have at least one copy of the mutant gene (30 percent have one copy and 2 percent have two copies). About 49 percent of miniature Australian Shepherds have at least one copy of it (45 percent have one copy and 4 percent have two copies).

4 **What other drugs can dogs with the MDR1 mutation be sensitive to?**

Other drugs that are known to be problematic:

* Abamectin, selamectin, milbemycin, and moxidectin: antiparasite agents used in heartworm, ear mite, mange mite, and yard preparations; at doses used to prevent heartworm, these drugs, as well as ivermectin, are safe in mutant MDR1 dogs, but at levels used to treat mange, they are not.
* Loperamide: antidiarrheal agent; not safe at normal doses.
* Acepromazine: tranquilizer; produces deeper and longer sedation.
* Butorphanol: analgesic and pre-anesthetic agent; produces deeper and longer sedation.
* Vincristine, vinblastine, and doxorubicin: chemotherapy agents; more likely to cause bone marrow suppression and gastrointestinal upset.
* Erythromycin: antibiotic used to combat bacterial infections; may cause neurological signs.

Some drugs are suspected to be pumped from the brain by the protein produced by the MDR1 gene but appear to be safe for dogs with the MDR1 mutation. These include cyclosporin (an immunosuppressive drug); digoxin (a heart drug); doxycycline (an antibacterial drug often prescribed for tick-borne diseases); and morphine, buprenorphine, and fentanyl (all opioid analgesics), among other less frequently prescribed drugs. Dogs with the MDR1 mutation that are prescribed these drugs should be monitored. For trade names under which these drugs are marketed, go to *www.busteralert.org*.

5 **Does the MDR1 mutation act as a dominant or recessive?**

It acts as an incomplete dominant. Dogs with one copy of the mutant gene are said to be sensitive; they may have toxic reactions to normal doses of loperamide and some anticancer drugs, and to high doses of ivermectin.

Dogs with two copies of the mutant gene are said to be super-sensitive; they are very likely to have toxic reactions to normal doses of loperamide and some anticancer drugs, and to high doses of ivermectin.

6 How do I know if my dog has the mutant MDR1 gene?

A DNA test is available from Washington State University. The test will determine if your dog has zero, one, or two copies of the MDR1 mutation. To get a test kit, go to *www.vetmed.wsu.edu/depts-VCPL/test.aspx*. The test requires a simple cheek swab and costs about $70.

7 Why should I find out?

Because several of the drugs that dogs with the mutation are sensitive to are commonly used for surgery, it's a good idea to find out now if your Aussie has the MDR1 gene. You can order a medic alert ID for your Aussie at *www.busteralert.org*.

If your Aussie has the MDR1 mutant gene, you should take the following precautions:

- Acepromazine and butorphanol: For dogs with one copy of the MDR1 mutant gene, reduce the dose by 25 percent; for dogs with two copies, reduce by 30 to 50 percent.
- Loperamide: Avoid even at normal doses—it causes neurological toxicity.
- Ivermectin: Safe when given at the approved dose (6 micrograms per kilogram) for heartworm prevention. It is not safe at the higher doses (300–600 micrograms per kilogram) used to treat mange, especially for those with two copies of the mutant gene.

- Selamectin, milbemycin, and moxidectin: These drugs are safe when used at the manufacturer's recommended dose. The higher dose (generally 10–20 times higher than the heartworm prevention dose) prescribed for treatment of mange or other mites should be avoided.
- Vincristine, vinblastine, and doxorubicin: These chemotherapy drugs, should be reduced by 25 to 30 percent.
- Erythromycin: Should be avoided or monitored.

8 Should dogs with the MDR1 mutation be bred?

Dogs with two copies of the mutant MDR1 gene should only be bred to dogs with no copies (so all the offspring only have one copy). Dogs with one copy should only be bred to dogs with just one copy (so only a quarter of the offspring will have two copies) or, preferably, to dogs with no copies.

9 Where did the gene come from?

DNA analysis suggests that the mutation occurred in Europe from 20 to 120 generations before the various breeds that now have it diverged in the late 1800s. Assuming an average generation time of four years, this would place the origin at some time after the fourteenth century.

10 Does the mutant gene cause any other problems?

As far as is known, the mutant MDR1 gene causes no problems except for specific drug toxicities.

Chapter Seven

Training and Activities

Australian Shepherds were born to *do*. More than almost any other breed, they need a job. They thrive on activity, especially if it involves both mental and physical effort. Without both, you'll find that your Aussie is unfulfilled, and your Aussie ownership unfulfilling.

Aussies can be just about anything—a skilled herder, talented obedience competitor, dazzling agility dog, courageous guardian, fun-loving playmate, and devoted companion—but they can't do it without guidance. Aussies want to be good, but they aren't born with an innate sense of what's right and what's wrong. You have to show them. Fortunately, most Aussies are apt pupils.

As active dogs, Aussies need training, but they learn exceedingly quickly. They pick up complex tasks and actually try to understand what you want. That doesn't mean they always succeed, however. Their active minds work against them at times, making commands such as *"heel"* and *"stay"* major challenges when their inner self is screaming "Jump!" and "Go!"

To combat the Aussie's notorious energy and distraction levels, you need to do a few things:

- Give your Aussie plenty of interactive exercise—not just before training, but every day—so that he's not overly excited when you spend time with him.
- Make following your commands so rewarding he'd rather do that than anything else. This means using lots of tasty treats, along with lots of praise. The way to an Aussie's brain is through his stomach!
- Teach your Aussie a cue that means he needs to focus on you. Have a bunch of treats handy, and when he looks at your face, say *"Good!"* and reward him. Soon he'll catch on that looking at you is likely to end up getting him a treat. At this point add a distraction by holding the treat away from you, to the side. He'll probably mostly look at it, but when he glances back at you, quickly say *"Good!"* and reward him. Work up gradually until he has to look at you for five seconds, even with the treat held to the side. When he's doing that reliably add the cue *"Watch me!"* just as he begins to turn toward you. Repeat that, then start rewarding him only when he looks to you after you have said *"Watch me!"* Finally, try it in more distracting situations.

Training Techniques

If it's been a while since you've trained a dog, you'll find that things have changed. In the old days military-style training, which emphasized force-based methods over reward-based methods, predominated. These days training is based on rewards, using techniques perfected in animal learning experiments and even dolphin-training shows. Training is more fun and much easier, and dogs try harder, when the motivation is to gain something good rather than to avoid something bad.

The old school of dog training warned that if you started training your dog with treats, you would have to give your dog treats forever or he would quit working. How can you avoid spending the rest of your life as a walking treat dispenser? The best way is to give treats sometimes, and to give praise all the time. So you'll either give praise and then a treat, or praise alone.

When you first teach him something, you'll want to reward him every time he does it right. But once he knows it, you can cut back gradually, rewarding him only some of the times, but still praising every time. Like a slot machine, you should pay off at random times, so he's always wondering if the next time he does something he'll hit the jackpot. You can add some extra-special jackpot rewards to the mix to really keep him working for them.

If you train your dog before his regular mealtime, he'll work much better for food. In fact, instead of giving treats in addition to your dog's regular food, you can dole out his dinner bit by bit as rewards during training ses-

FYI: Heavy-Duty Arsenal

If you simply can't control your Aussie using a regular collar and rewards, there are ways to exert more control.

A popular option is a prong collar, a slip (actually martingale) collar with metal prongs all around its inside perimeter. When the collar is tightened the prongs poke through the dog's thick coat and pinch into his neck somewhat. The jab gets the dog's attention better than a standard slip collar. Because these collars have the potential to be painful, you must only use them under the supervision of an experienced trainer.

A preferable option is a head halter, which fits around the dog's head and muzzle. By controlling the head much as you would a horse's head, you can better control the direction the dog is going. When the dog pulls against a collar, he is able to pull in a straight line and get his weight behind it. When he pulls against a head halter, it turns his head back toward you so he can never pull in a straight line or get his weight behind it. Because a head halter gives you so much control, you do have to be careful that you are not wrenching the dog's head back and forth.

Finally, electric collars are sometimes suggested. The best use of such collars is to dissuade a dog from doing something enticing but wrong, such as chasing livestock, when he is out of arm's reach.

sions. If you're in a hurry, just train for a few minutes, give a few rewards, and then give a jackpot of his entire meal.

Training Equipment

You don't need a lot of equipment to get started. You can use either a buckle or slip (choke) collar. If you use a slip collar, remember the right way to put it on: As you are facing the dog, the collar should be in the shape of a "*P*," with the dog's head put through the loop in the "P." If you put it on backwards, it won't release after it's been tightened.

You'll also want a 4- to 6-foot (about 1- to 2-m) long leash, in any material except chain. Later, you'll want a 15- to 20-foot (about 4.5- to 6-m) line for training the *come* command.

Your most important training tool, next to your sense of humor, is a stash of tiny treats for rewards. You can use kibble (cat food kibble is seen as a special treat), cheese, tiny pieces of hot dog, or just about anything your Aussie can down in one gulp.

You may also want a clicker, a small device available at pet stores that makes a distinctive click sound when you press it.

The Trick of the Click

Many progressive obedience instructors and animal trainers use clicker training. A click is merely a signal that you use to help tell your dog when he's doing something right. It's a distinctive noise that takes the place of

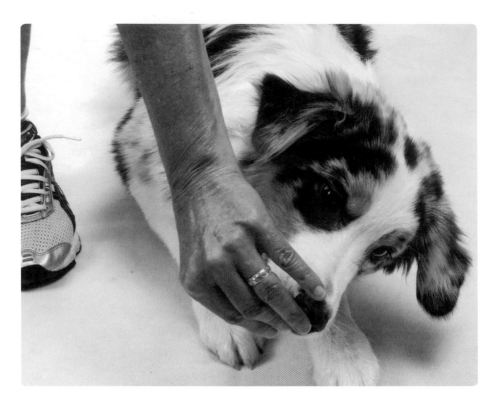

saying "*Good!*" to mark the instant when your dog is doing what you want. It works better than the word "*Good!*" because your dog notices an unusual sound (in this case, a click) more than he notices your words. You can buy a clicker at a pet supply store, or use anything that makes a distinctive sound.

By following the click sound with a reward, your dog quickly learns that the click means "Yes, that's it!" Because the click is faster and shorter than your voice, it can more precisely mark the moment your dog is doing something right. The click also tells the dog he can end the behavior, so once you click, don't expect him to continue sitting or doing whatever you've been teaching him. Once he understands how to do something, you can phase out the click, but not the praise and rewards.

To start clicker training, you'll want lots of tiny treats. You can start by simply clicking and then giving your dog a treat so he learns that a click means a treat is coming. You'll need to do this at least 20 times before he'll start to look at your treat hand expectantly after he hears the click. Once you start training, remember:

- Give a click instantly when your dog does what you want. The faster you click, the easier it is for him to figure out what you like.
- Give a reward as soon as you can after the click.

In this chapter, substitute your clicker sound anywhere it says to use the word "*Good!*"

Instruction

You may be able to hire someone to train your dog, but unless you're setting your sights on advanced herding work, you should be able to do almost any training yourself—as long as you have a good teacher. Training classes are a way to receive training instruction, practice what you've learned at home, and make friends with other dog owners and their dogs. The best classes use reward-based techniques. You may be able to find one through a local obedience club (go to *www.akc.org*, and click on "Clubs," then "Club Search"), through recommendations from local Aussie clubs, through your veterinarian, or through the Association of Pet Dog Trainers (*www.aptd.com*).

Don't wait until your Aussie is an adult, or even an older puppy, to get started. Dogs that are exposed to learning at a young age are much more adept at learning new things as adults. Puppy kindergarten classes are generally open to dogs between the ages of 12 weeks and 6 months. Kindergarten classes allow puppies to learn to learn, and to socialize with other dogs and people in a structured setting. They help your dog learn to enjoy going places with you and to become a well-behaved member of public gatherings that include other dogs. They provide a setting in which to teach new skills and cope with budding behavior problems under the supervision of an experienced instructor. Look for classes that emphasize reward-based training using play, toys, and treats. Avoid classes that advocate physical punishment, chain choke collars, neck scruffing, shaking, or alpharolls (in which you force the puppy on his back and hold him there until he submits).

Breed Needs

Training Tips

- Train in gradual steps. Give rewards for getting closer and closer to the final behavior. Be patient!
- Give your dog feedback ("*Good!*") instantly when he does what you want. The faster you mark the behavior like this, the easier it is for your dog to figure out what you like. Think of it as taking a picture of the moment to show to the dog and say "Do this again!"
- Give a reward as soon as you can after saying "*Good!*"
- Don't forget to praise your dog as part of the reward!
- Don't start using a cue word ("*Sit,*" "*Down,*" and the like) until your dog knows the behavior.
- Just say a cue word once. Repeating it over and over won't help your dog learn it.
- Teach new behaviors in a quiet place away from distractions. Only when your dog knows the behavior very well should you gradually start practicing it in other places.
- Don't train your dog if you're impatient or mad. You won't be able to hide your frustration.
- Dogs learn better in short sessions. Train your Aussie for only about 10 to 15 minutes at a time. Always quit while he's still having fun. You can train him several times a day if you want.

ACTIVITIES A Handy Trick

One of the easiest ways to teach your dog new things is to teach him to target, in which his task is to follow your hand with his nose on command. Once he's learned it, you can essentially lead him around by the nose without using a leash or a treat. It's easy to teach:

1. Rub a tiny bit of sticky food, such as cheese or liverwurst, on your hand, and have your dog sniff it. When he touches your hand, say "*Good*" and let him lick it off.
2. Repeat this step, gradually moving your hand so he has to follow it before touching it.
3. Add the command "*Touch*" before showing your hand to him.
4. Transfer the food from your hand to your other hand. He must now touch the empty hand before being rewarded with the treat from your other hand.
5. Use the *touch* command and your hand to lure your dog into position as you train other exercises. For example, to train him in *heel* position, keep your hand by your side so he's in the proper place. To teach *come*, call out "*Come*" and then hold up your hand and say "*Touch!*" He should come running to your hand.

Adults and older puppies will profit from more advanced classes. Again, look for reward-based training methods. Classes are a great impetus to keep you on a training schedule, and most Aussies are class leaders. But don't be too concerned if your dog isn't the head of the class. All dogs learn at different rates and learn some things more easily than others. Your Aussie may be especially excited by the commotion of class, which is all the more reason he needs to be there!

Even without a class, you can still teach your Aussie the basics: how to *heel*, *sit*, *down*, *stay*, and *come*.

Training the Basics

Aussies are capable of amazing feats of obedience, but start with the basics of walking on leash, sitting, staying, coming, and lying down.

Leash Walking

Leash walking is often the pup's introduction to formal training. Traditional trainers often advocate dragging the dog until he tires of fighting the leash, but there's no need for that. Here's what you do:

1. Place a buckle collar on the puppy and attach a leash. Give him a treat.
2. Lure him forward with a treat and give it to him. Keep luring him forward a little more as you walk slowly along with him at your side. Give him a treat every few steps.
3. If he wants to go in a different direction, or stops and bucks, go ahead and walk in his direction a few steps before trying to lure him along again. If he absolutely refuses to move, carry him a short distance away and see if he'll walk back with you to some place he wants to go.
4. As he gets better, you can ignore him when he's stopping, being sure to reward him as soon as he lets the leash get slack.
5. If he pulls ahead on the leash, dragging you, stop dead in your tracks. Don't pull back; just stand there. Only when he lets the leash go slack do you say "*Good!*" and reward or move forward. Practice this until he stops pulling as soon as you stop.
6. Next, walk toward something he wants to reach. If he pulls, stop or even back up. The point is not to jerk your dog back but to show him that pulling gets him there more slowly. When he stops pulling go toward the goal again. The goal is his reward, but the only way he can reach it is to stop pulling!

Heeling

Most of the time you'll be content that your Aussie walks on a leash without pulling or lunging, but there are times when you'd like him to stay right at your side in *heel* position. Technically, that position is on your left side, with your dog's neck level with your leg. Here's how to teach your dog to heel:

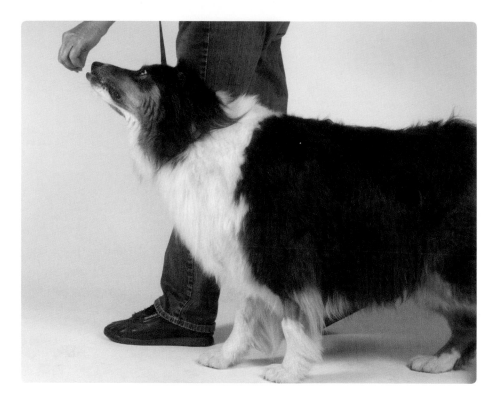

1. Use a treat to maneuver your dog into *heel* position. Once he is there say *"Good!"* and reward him.
2. Eventually you can start to use the stick without a treat, bending down and rewarding him from your hand, and then get rid of the stick altogether.
3. Next add the cue: *"Heel!"*
4. After he is heeling while you walk calmly, make staying in *heel* position a game by running and turning, and rewarding when he is able to stick to your side. Have him sit every time you stop, until he does so automatically. Reinforce the idea of *heel* position by having him sit, then turn with you as you pivot 90 or 180 degrees, and have him sit again. Or take just one step forward or to the side, and have him *heel* and sit with you. You can even teach him to reverse!

Sitting on Command

You can teach a dog to sit in many ways, but one of the easiest is to lure him into sitting, as follows:

1. Hold a treat just above and behind the level of his eyes. If he bends his knees and points his nose up, tell him *"Good!"* and reward him. If instead he walks backward, practice with his rear end a few inches from a corner to prevent him from backing up.

2. Repeat this several times, each time moving the treat further back, until finally your dog's butt is touching the ground.
3. Next, repeat the exercise without a treat, using only your hand to guide him. When he sits, give him a treat from your other hand.
4. Gradually abbreviate your hand movements until you are only using a small hand signal.
5. When he is sitting reliably add the verbal cue "*Sit!*" right before the hand signal. The verbal signal will come to predict the hand signal, and he will soon learn to sit to either.

Lying Down on Command

To teach your dog to lie down on command:

1. Have him sit; then show him a treat and move it forward and downward.
2. If his elbows touch the ground, say "*Good!*" and reward him. Even if he only goes partway, reward him. Then repeat, rewarding for going down farther. If he keeps trying to get up, you can place your hands over his shoulders to help guide him downward.
3. Next, repeat but without a treat in the hand you have been using to lure him. When he sits, give him a treat from your other hand.
4. Gradually abbreviate your hand movements until you are only using a small hand signal.
5. Add the verbal cue "*Down*" right before the hand signal.

Staying When Told

The *stay* command is one of the hardest for an Aussie to master, so be prepared to go in small steps. Because staying is essentially asking the dog to do nothing, it's taught by introducing the cue word "*Stay*" right from the start. Otherwise he wouldn't know the difference between a *sit* or *down* when you forget to reward him and this new behavior of not moving. Here's how to teach your Aussie to stay:

1. Cue your dog to sit. Say "*Stay*" and hold your palm in a stop signal in front of his face. Wait for a few seconds, then reward him and say "*OK!*"
2. Tell him to stay, give him the stop signal, and then pivot out in front of him. If your dog is having a problem getting the concept, you can have him sit on a raised surface or behind a small barrier so it's more difficult for him to move. Always be sure to reward him before you give him the "*OK!*" signal.
3. Work up gradually to a longer duration. If he gets up, simply put him back in position and start over, decreasing the duration you expect of him.
4. Next work on moving to different positions around your dog, still remaining close to him. Move in front, to either side, and behind your dog, and gradually move farther away. Keeping a finger on the top of his head as you pivot around him may help at first.
5. Introduce mild distractions, gradually working to greater ones. Remember, you want your dog to succeed!

Coming When Called

Here's how to teach a reliable *come* on command:

1. You will need a friend to help you, and a long hallway or other enclosed area. Have your helper hold your dog while you back away, showing your dog a treat or toy.
2. The dog should be pulling and whining to get to you and the reward. Once he is, your helper should release him so he can run to you. You can even turn and run away to increase your puppy's enthusiasm. Say "*Good!*" the moment he touches you, and then quickly reward him.
3. Eventually you want to be able to touch his collar so that you don't end up with a dog that dances around just outside your reach. To do that, wait until you touch or hold his collar before rewarding him.
4. Once he is running to you reliably, add the cue "*Come!*" just before your helper releases him. Practice this several times for many sessions.
5. Once he is coming on cue, let him meander around on his own. Call "*Come*" and reward him when he lets you touch his collar.
6. Finally, practice in lots of different places, gradually choosing places with more distractions. Keep your dog on a long light line for his safety.

Always make coming to you rewarding. If you want your dog to come so you can give him a bath or put him to bed or do anything else he doesn't really like, go get him rather than call him. Practice calling him when outdoors or around the house, giving him a reward, and then leaving him on his own again.

Tricks

Aussies love to learn. They'll master the basics with ease, then look for other challenges. Teaching your Aussie new tricks throughout his life will go far in keeping him mentally stimulated. Use the same training methods you used to teach him the basic commands; that is, go gradually, luring him if possible, rewarding for partial successes, and using lots of rewards. If your Aussie can do it, you can teach him to do it.

Shake Hands

Here's a great trick to break the ice!

1. Kneel facing your sitting dog.
2. Reach for his right paw with your right hand. He may naturally give you his paw, but if he doesn't, use a treat to lure his head way to the left, so he's almost looking over his shoulder. That will make his right paw lift. Praise and reward him as soon as his paw goes up.
3. Keep repeating, until he starts lifting his paw on his own.
4. Add the cue *"How do you do?"* and only give him your hand and reward him when he shakes on cue.

Speak

Although it may seem like teaching your Aussie to bark is the last thing you want to do, it's actually handy as a first step in teaching him to be quiet.

1. Figure out what makes him bark. The best situation is if he barks at you to urge you to give him a treat. Once he barks, say *"Good!"* and reward him.
2. Introduce the cue word (*"Speak!"*) quickly for this trick. You don't want to reward him for speaking out of turn!
3. Once you've introduced the cue word, never reward him for speaking on his own. In fact, introduce a new command, *"Shhhh,"* and reward him only for not barking.

Fun Facts

Jay Sisler's Amazing Aussies

In the 1950s, Jay Sisler's performing Aussies were seen by thousands of people at rodeos all over the country. Sisler's techniques were more like those of modern trainers than those fashionable in his day. He trained a dog for 10 to 15 minutes three times a day, concentrating on only one thing at a time. He didn't use a leash and preferred to lead them rather than force them into doing what he wanted. He used hotcakes for rewards. If a dog had a hard time on a particular trick, he'd lay off training that trick for a couple of months and then come back to it. He taught his dogs to jump rope, play leapfrog, walk on their front or hind legs, balance on bars, stand on their heads, and more. For a sampling of what Aussies can do, check out Sisler's two home movies available on *www.youtube.com* by searching for "Jay Sisler."

Obedience and Tracking Trials

Chances are your Aussie makes the grade when it comes to learning. You can show off his sharp mind and manners at a variety of tests and competitions sponsored by the AKC and ASCA. Some take just a little training, while others require intensive training to succeed.

The Good Shepherd

A major goal of your training will be to have your dog behave in public. The AKC has outlined a series of exercises your dog should master to be a good public citizen. The AKC also offers a simple test (on leash) where he can demonstrate his proficiency and earn the Canine Good Citizenship (CGC) title. To earn the title he will be asked to

- Accept a friendly stranger without acting shy or resentful, or breaking position to approach; sit politely for petting and allow the stranger to examine his ears, feet, and coat, and to brush him.
- Walk politely on a loose leash, turning and stopping with you, walking through a group of at least three other people without jumping on them, pulling, or acting overly exuberant, shy, or resentful. He need not be perfectly aligned with you, but he shouldn't be pulling.
- Sit and lie down on command (you can gently guide him into position) and then stay as you walk 20 feet away and back.
- Stay and then come to you when called from 10 feet away.
- Behave politely to another dog-and-handler team, showing only casual interest in them.
- React calmly to distractions, such as a dropped chair or passing jogger, without panicking, barking, or acting aggressively.
- Remain calm when held by a stranger while you're out of sight for three minutes.
- Refrain from eliminating, growling, snapping, biting, or attempting to attack a person or dog throughout the evaluation.

Go to *www.akc.org/events/cgc* to learn more about the CGC test or find out where one is being held.

Rally Obedience

A step up in difficulty from the CGC test is the Novice Rally Obedience competition, followed in turn by slightly more difficult Rally competition levels. Rally is a great way to get involved in obedience sports because it's fairly low key and a lot of fun! Both the AKC and ASCA offer Rally competitions.

In rally, you and your Aussie walk through a course consisting of 10 to 20 signs, each with instructions telling you which exercise to perform. Some of the exercises are moving exercises, such heeling at various paces, turning, circling, stepping to one side, or calling your dog to you. Others are stationary exercises, such as having your dog lie down, stay, or pivot in heel position. You can talk to your dog throughout, praise him, and repeat commands, but you can't pull him along on his leash, touch him, or carry treats or toys. Points are deducted for mistakes, but scoring emphasizes teamwork more than precision.

Each course is different, and you won't get to see it until you arrive at the trial. That means you'll need to know all the possible exercises, even though

ACTIVITIES Rally Signs and Titles

AKC Class	Title	Leash	Number of Signs	Stationary Exercises	Jumps	Exercises
Novice	RN	on	10–15	no more than 5	0	basic list
Advanced	RA	off	12–17	no more than 7	1	Novice plus pivots, call front, stand
Excellent	RE	off	15–20	no more than 7	1–2	Advanced plus reverse, moving stand, honor

you'll only be asked to do some of them. For AKC Novice, the basic exercises are:

- *Halt* and *sit* or *down*
- 90-degree, 270-degree, and 360-degree right and left turns
- Right and left circles
- Call front from *heel*; then finish back to *heel* position from right or left
- Heel at normal, slow, and fast paces
- Moving sidestep to right
- Spiral with dog to inside and outside
- Weave around four pylons one or both ways
- Halt, take one step forward and halt (dog sits), two steps forward and halt, three steps forward and halt
- Call to front (dog sits), take one step backward and call dog to front again, two steps calling dog to front, three steps calling dog to front
- Walk around dog in *sit-stay* position and *down-stay* position

More advanced classes include low jumps; 90- and 180-degree pivots to either direction in which the dog stays in *heel* position at your side as you pivot, the dog starting and finishing in a sit; and an honor exercise, in which the dog remains in a *sit* or *down* position at the edge of the ring while another dog goes through the course. The honoring (staying) dog is on leash.

Each exercise has a particular sign with symbols that describe it and each exercise has a particular way it should be performed. To find out more and see signs, go to *www.rallyobedience.com*.

To earn a title, a dog must qualify three times at that level. The most advanced AKC title, Rally Advanced Excellent (RAE), is awarded to dogs that qualify ten times in both the Advanced class and the Excellent class at the same trial.

Formal Obedience

In these trials, you can't talk or gesture to your dog except to give commands, and you can only praise between exercises. Instead of printed directions, a judge tells you what to do as you go along. You get few, if any, second chances, and precision counts. Both the AKC and the ASCA offer similar titles, with similar exercises at each level.

The Novice Obedience class consists of:

- Heeling on and off leash, with the dog sitting automatically each time you stop; negotiating right, left, and about turns, and changing to a faster and slower pace
- Heeling on leash in a figure eight around two people
- Standing off lead without moving while the judge touches him
- Waiting for you to call and then coming from about 20 feet (about 6 meters) away, returning to *heel* position on command
- Staying in a *sit* position for one minute, and then a *down* position for three minutes, in a group of other dogs while you are 20 feet (about 6 meters) away

If your dog passes three times, he earns the Companion Dog (CD) title.

The Open Obedience class consists of:

- Heeling, including a figure eight, off leash
- Coming when called as in Novice, except dropping to a *down* position when told to do so about halfway back to you, and then continuing the recall when commanded
- Retrieving a thrown dumbbell first over flat ground and then over a jump
- Jumping over a broad jump
- Staying in a *sit* position for three minutes, and then a *down* position for five minutes, in a group of other dogs while you are out of view

If your dog passes three times, he earns the Companion Dog Excellent (CDX) title.

The Utility Obedience class consists of:

- Heeling, coming, standing, sitting, downing, and staying in response to hand signals
- Allowing the judge to touch him while the handler is 10 feet (3 meters) away
- Retrieving a leather, and then a metal, article scented by the handler from a group of similar unscented articles
- Retrieving one of three gloves designated by the handler
- Trotting away from the handler until told to stop and turn around 40 feet (12 meters) away, jumping the designated jump, and returning to the handler. This is then repeated, jumping the opposite jump.

If your dog passes three times, he earns the Utility Dog (UD) title.

The Utility Dog Excellent (UDX) title is awarded for qualifying in both Open and Utility classes on the same day at 10 trials. A number after the UDX indicates how many times the dog has fulfilled these requirements. One Aussie earned a UDX 23, indicating she qualified in both classes at least 230 times!

Obedience Trial Champion (OTCH) is the supreme obedience title, requiring a dog to earn 100 points, plus three first placements, by scoring better than other qualifying dogs in Open or Utility. An OTCH is a rarity in most breeds, but it's almost—but not quite—common in Aussies!

High in Trial (HIT) is awarded to the top scorer of the day at an obedience trial. Aussies are frequently top contenders for High in Trial.

Tracking

Following a scent trail is one of the most mystifying abilities of dogs, but most of them need a little help with perfecting the technique and doing it on command. The best time to teach is in the very early morning, when some dew is still on the ground, because it holds scent better. Find an area you haven't walked over recently and, without your dog, walk a short distance, dropping treats along the trail. Then go get him and let him follow from treat to treat. Repeat the process in another fresh area, dropping the treats slightly farther apart. Eventually he'll figure out he can find the treats by following your scent trails, and you can leave a cache of treat treasure at the end of the trail instead of dropping them along the way.

You can also simply hide from him, assuming he wants to find you! This works best if you have a helper hold him while you go hide, walking over fresh ground and hiding in a bush or other covered area. Greet him with lots of praise and a few treats!

Both the AKC and the ASCA offer tracking titles your Aussie can earn. The requirements are essentially the same in both, but the ASCA does not offer the VST title.

ACTIVITIES Tracking Titles

AKC Title	Track Length	Turns	Track Age	Surface
Tracking Dog (TD)	440–500 yards	3–5	0.5–2 hours	natural
Tracking Dog Excellent (TDX)	800–1000 yards	5–7	3–5 hours	varied natural
Variable Surface (VST)	600–800 yards	4–8	3–5 hours	varied natural and manmade

A Champion Tracker (CT) title is awarded to a dog that has earned the TD, TDX, and VST titles.

For more information visit *www.akc.org/events/tracking*.

Agility Trials

If you like your activities a little more active than heeling and such, agility competition may be what you're looking for—and almost certainly what your Aussie would vote for! Agility is an adrenaline-amping obstacle course for dogs run against the clock, combining jumping, climbing, weaving, running, zipping through tunnels, and loads of fun.

Several organizations, including the AKC, the ASCA, the United Kennel Club (UKC), the North American Dog Agility Council (NADAC), and the United States Dog Agility Association (USDAA), sponsor trials and award titles, each with slightly different flavors of agility. The ASCA offers three titling classes: Regular, Jumpers, and Gamblers, with Novice, Open, and Elite levels in each. The AKC program is described here, but don't discount the others, which many competitors find to be even more fun.

AKC agility trials feature a variety of obstacles:

- The A-frame is made of two 8- or 9-feet (2.4- or 2.7-m) long boards each 3 to 4 feet (about 1 m) wide, leaned against each other so they form an A-frame with the peak 5 to 5.5 feet (1.5 to 1.7 m) off the ground. The dog runs up one side and down the other.

- The Dog Walk is either an 8- or 12-foot (2.4- or 3.6-m) long and 1-foot (30-cm) wide board that is either 3 or 4 feet (about 1 m) high, suspended between two like boards that lead up to it on one side and down from it on the other. The dog runs up one plank, over the horizontal plank, and down the other plank.
- The Teeter is a seesaw with a 12-foot (3.6-m) plank. The dog runs up one side until his weight causes the teeter to shift so the dog can walk down the other side.
- The Pause Table is about 3 feet (about 1 m) square. The dog has to jump up on it, then either sit or lie down as commanded for five seconds.
- The Open Tunnel is a flexible tube, from 10 to 20 feet (3 to 6 m) in length and about 2 feet (61 cm) in diameter. It is often bent into an S or C shape for the dog to run through.
- The Chute is a rigid barrel with a lightweight fabric chute about 12 to 15 feet (3.6 to 4.6 m) long attached to one end. The dog runs into the open end of the barrel and continues blindly through the collapsed chute until he comes out the other end.

- The Weave Poles are a series of from 6 to 12 vertical poles spaced 20 to 24 inches (51 to 61 cm) apart. The dog takes a serpentine route, weaving from one side of the poles to the other.
- The Jumps consist of single-bar, panel, double-bar, and triple-bar jumps. The double and triples are both wide and tall. The bars are easily displaced, making it safe when a dog fails to clear them. The dog must jump without knocking any bars down.
- The Tire Jump is about 2 feet (61 cm) in diameter, with the bottom of the opening at the same height as the other jumps. The dog must jump through the opening.
- The Broad Jump is a spaced series of four to five slightly raised boards.

AKC agility is divided into two types of courses. The Standard course includes all the obstacle types, including those referred to as contact obstacles: the Λ-frame, Dog Walk, Teeter, and Pause Table. The Jumpers With Weaves (JWW) course includes only jumps, tunnels, and weaves, usually in a somewhat more intricate course pattern than the Standard.

The **Novice** Standard class uses 12 to 13 obstacles, and the Novice JWW class uses 13 to 15 obstacles. The obstacles are set up in a fairly straightforward course. Dogs that qualify three times earn the Novice Agility (NA) or Novice Agility Jumpers (NAJ) title, respectively.

The **Open** Standard class uses 15 to 17 obstacles, and the Open JWW class uses 16 to 18 obstacles, set up in a trickier pattern than in Novice. Dogs that qualify three times earn the Open Agility (OA) or Open Agility Jumpers (OAJ) title, respectively.

Both **Excellent** standard classes use 18 to 20 obstacles, set up in a very challenging pattern. Dogs that qualify three times earn the Agility Excellent (AX) or Agility Excellent Jumpers (AXJ) title. Dogs that continue to compete in Excellent, and earn 10 additional qualifying scores by finishing the course in a slightly shorter time than required for the AX and AXJ titles, earn the Master Agility (MA) and Master Agility Jumpers (MAJ) titles. The Master Agility Champion (MACH) title requires qualifying at 20 trials in both Standard and Jumpers Excellent classes, and earning 750 points. One point is earned for each second under the allotted course time in which the dog completes the course. Dogs can earn a MACH2 title, and so on, for repeating the requirements. In 2007, a miniature Australian Shepherd named MACH8 Blue Moon Shine On Willow won the National Agility Champion title in the 12" jump division.

Herding and Stockdog Trials

Many Aussie owners find that the most exciting Aussie sport is the one the dogs were bred for—namely, herding or stockdog competitions. The AKC offers herding tests and trials. Tests generally refer to noncompetitive events in which dogs must exhibit a certain level of proficiency to pass; trials

FYI: Stockdog and Herding Titles

The following titles are offered by the different organizations sponsoring herding and stockdog tests or trials. (Note: Several titles are seen in conjunction with the lowercase letters s, c, or d. These denote that the title was earned with either sheep, cattle, or ducks.)

The ASCA offers the following stockdog titles:

- Started Trial Dog (STD), Open Trial Dog (OTD), and Advanced Trial Dog (ATD) represent progressively more demanding trial titles. The Working Trial Championship (WTCh) is awarded when the ATD is earned with all three eligible stock species (sheep, cattle, and ducks).
- Post-Advanced Trial Dog (PATD) requires working stock in a large field.
- Ranch Trial Dog (RTD) is awarded based on performance with sheep, goats, or cattle in a ranch setting. It includes pen work, sorting work, chute work, and pasture work, in which the pasture is at least 5 acres.
- Ranch Dog (RD) certification is earned by dogs working stock at home. The dog must regularly work stock as an aid to his owner's livelihood. More advanced certifications of Ranch Dog Good (RDG) and Ranch Dog Excellent (RDX) are also awarded.

The AKC offers the following herding titles:

- Herding Test (HT) and Pre-Trial (PT) are noncompetitive titles based on the display of basic herding instinct and ability.
- Herding Started (HS), Herding Intermediate (HI), and Herding Excellent (HX) represent progressively more demanding titles. Three qualifying scores are required for each title.

- Herding Championships (HCh) require earning placements in the most advanced level after completing the HX title.

Three types of courses are available: The "A" course requires working stock through obstacles and penning within an arena; the "B" course requires an outrun, lift, fetch, pen, and (for an HX), a shed; and the "C" course is performed with larger flocks in more open areas.

The American Herding Breed Association (AHBA) offers the following titles:

Tests:

- The Herding Capability Test (HCT) consists of a test of basic instinct and basic stock moving abilities.
- The Junior Herding Dog (JHD) Test consists of a simple course ending in a fence-line pen.

Earning these titles requires two qualifying scores using either sheep, goats, ducks, geese, or sometimes cattle.

Trials:

- Herding Trial Dog (HTD) trials include three successively more difficult levels (I, II, and III), all of which include an outrun, lift, fetch, drive, and pen.
- Herding Ranch Dog (HRD) trials include a greater variety of elements and tasks more like those a working stockdog might actually encounter.

Earning these titles requires two qualifying scores using either sheep, goats, ducks (except for HRD), geese, or cattle.

- Herding Trial Championship (HTCh) is awarded to dogs that earn 10 additional qualifying scores after completing the HTD III or HRD III titles.

usually denote competitive events in which dogs are scored and placed in relation to one another. The ASCA offers stockdog trials.

It would be extremely difficult to train your dog to herd on your own. For starters, you'd need your own sheep and training pen. But mostly, you need the advice of an experienced stockdog trainer. If possible, attend a herding or stockdog trial and ask if any trainers live close to you. Most hard-core competitors run and train Border Collies, not Aussies, but as long as they don't expect your Aussie to work the same way that a Border Collie works, they should be able to help you and your dog.

More Fun Sports

Not all dog sports are sanctioned by the AKC or ASCA, but that doesn't mean they're any less fun. Two Aussie favorites are Flyball and flying disc competitions.

Flyball

Flyball is the sport for adrenaline junkies. It's a series of relay races in which dogs run a short course with four low jumps placed every 10 feet along it, hitting a box at one end that triggers a ball, catching the ball, and turning to race back down the lane to their handlers. Dogs run in relay teams of four, and the returning dog and starting dog cross the start/finish line at almost the same time. Aussies are the third most popular pure breed in the sport, behind Border Collies and Jack Russell Terriers. Two organizations sponsor competitions and titles: the North American Flyball Association (*www.flyballdogs.com*) and the United Flyball League International (*www.u-fli.com*).

Flying Disc Competitions

If your Aussie is a disc-catching wonder, you can compete in various canine disc-catching competitions. In Freestyle competition, competitors are judged on their teamwork, originality, and athletic agility as they spin and leap to great heights in pursuit of the flying disc. In Mini-Distance competition, the dog is scored on how many catches he makes in one minute, with scoring weighted by distance and height of the catch. Not surprisingly, Aussies excel at the sport.

Helpful Hints

Search Out a Resource

National Disaster Search Dog Foundation: *www.ndsdf.org*

National Association for Search & Rescue: *www.nasar.org/nasar/specialty_fields.php*

SAR dog organizations by state: *www.netpets.org/dogs/dogsar.html*

Search Dog Network: *www.searchdogs.org*

U.K. National Search and Rescue Dog Association: *www.nsarda.org.uk*

Service Activities

Many Aussies and their owners get the most satisfaction out of helping others, whether it's finding a missing person or comforting a sick child.

Search and Rescue Dogs

Search and rescue (SAR) Aussies may search for hikers lost in the wilds, children lost in the neighborhood, victims buried in the rubble of a collapsed building, skiers buried in an avalanche, or human remains underwater, underground, or scattered about. Each of these searches requires a different set of skills, and SAR dogs train extensively to be certified in areas such as Wilderness Searching, Urban Disaster, Avalanche, Article Work, Water Work, and Cadaver.

Some SAR dogs specialize in tracking, whereas others specialize in air scenting. Tracking dogs usually follow the scent trail of a particular person, usually someone who was last seen in a particular place, so the dog has a starting point. The dog may be given a sample of the person's scent. Air scenting dogs detect any human scent on air currents and follow it to its source. They are used in areas where unknown victims may be buried or no starting place for a track is known.

Aussies are a good breed for SAR work. They are athletic, large enough to be sturdy, and small enough to be agile. They have a double coat that allows them to work in extreme weather. They have good noses and naturally use them. But it's not their physical attributes that separate them from the crowd. Their natural inclination to please people, meet challenges, and keep trying is what really sets them apart. Their responsiveness and ability to follow directions is a must when working off-lead. They aren't aggressive to people or other dogs, and they don't tend to be incorrigible wildlife chasers.

One famous SAR Aussie named Ranger went on more than 100 missions, saving four lives, locating three bodies, finding a murder weapon, and helping locate a kidnapped child.

It takes about two years of daily training to ready an SAR dog for action. A puppy can begin to learn commands, how to handle his body in various situations, and how to use his nose. Begin by finding a canine SAR unit near you. You can start your search on the Internet or try calling your local sheriff's office. Attend a training session with the unit just to observe.

Therapy and Service Dogs

Aussies lift your spirits, make you laugh, and are medicine for the mind. That's why they are popular as therapy dogs, visiting people in nursing homes, children in hospitals, and homebound neighbors who relish the chance to interact with a dog.

Therapy dogs must be extensively socialized so that people who may act unpredictably don't upset them. They must pass a test that includes obedience (usually a Canine Good Citizen test); the ability to leave food, toys, and medications alone when working; the ability to tolerate being petted all over; and the willingness to greet strangers. Tricks come in handy as ice breakers. Some tricks, such as placing the front paws up on the side of a bed or chair on command, make it easier for a person to reach the dog for petting. Several certifying organizations exist, but the two largest ones in North America are Therapy Dogs International (*www.tdi-dog.org*) and the Delta Society (*www.deltasociety.org*).

Helpful Hints

Service Dog Organizations

Assistance Dogs International:
www.adionline.org

Dogs for the Deaf:
www.dogsforthedeaf.org

International Association of Assistance Dog Partners:
www.iaadp.org

Love on a Leash:
www.loveonaleash.org

Aussies can do even more than raise spirits; they can help people with disabilities by acting as service dogs. They may retrieve dropped items for people who can't bend over, pull a wheelchair, alert hearing-impaired owners to doorbells or alarms, act as seizure-alert dogs, or work as guides for the blind.

Leash Training

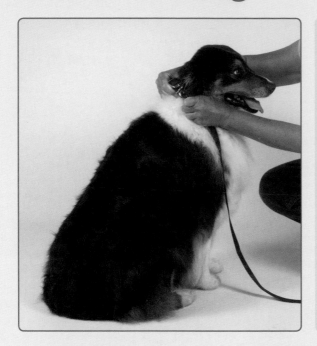

1 Place a leash on the puppy and, without pulling on it, lure him forward a step or two with a treat. Give him the treat. Keep luring him forward a little more as you walk slowly along with him at your side, giving him a treat every few steps.

2 If he wants to go in a different direction, let him lead for a few steps before trying to lure him along again.

3 If he refuses to move, pick him up and carry him away a few steps; then put him down and start over.

4 If he pulls ahead on the leash, dragging you, just stop. Only when he lets the leash go slack do you say "*Good!*" and reward or move forward.

The Sit Command

1 With him sitting with his back to a corner, hold a treat just above and behind the level of his eyes. If he bends his knees and points his nose up, say *"Good!"* and give him the treat.

2 The next time, move the treat farther back so he has to bend his legs more to get it. Keep repeating and moving it back until he's sitting. Be sure to tell him he's good right away and give him the treat each time.

3 Now guide him using just your hand with no treat. When he sits, give him a treat from your other hand.

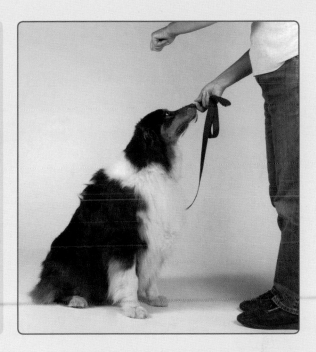

4 Gradually abbreviate your hand movements until you are only using a small hand signal. Then add the verbal signal *"Sit!"* right before the hand signal. Keep practicing and rewarding him.

139

The Stay Command

1 Have him sit beside you, and then say *"Stay"* while holding your palm in a stop signal in front of his face. If he gets up, simply put him back in position and start over, decreasing the duration you expect of him. Wait for a few seconds, then reward him and say *"OK!"*

2 After he's doing this reliably, do it again—except this time, pivot so you're standing facing him. Wait for a few seconds, then reward him and say *"OK!"*

3 Next work on moving around so you are on either side of and even behind your dog; then gradually increase the distance, and then the time.

4 Introduce mild distractions, and then practice in other locations. Keep him on a long line if you're anywhere he could get loose.

Chapter Eight

Grooming an Australian Shepherd

A ny Aussie owner will tell you the same thing: Maintaining an Aussie's coat takes little effort. Maintaining your home as well as an Aussie's coat takes considerably more effort, however!

Aussies don't tend to mat much, their hair doesn't need trimming, and dirt tends to fall from their coats. The problem is, the coat tends to fall from their bodies! Along with the dirt that has fallen from the coat, the fur accumulates on your floors. Your main line of defense—aside from a powerful vacuum cleaner—is diligent brushing to remove loose hair and dirt before it makes it into your house. But to really control shedding, you need to start with a bath.

Managing Shedding

You can't prevent your Aussie from shedding. You can, however, cut down on how much hair is shed in your house by getting as much loose hair out when you bathe and brush as possible. Bathing your Aussie will loosen any hair that would normally loosen on its own in the next week or so. Bathing in warm water is more effective at loosening hair than is bathing in cool water. Special de-shedding shampoos can also help in loosening hairs that are almost ready to go. Using a powerful spray and massaging the coat down to the skin will help dislodge hairs as well. Finally, drying with a high-velocity hair dryer can further help dislodge hairs, and certain brushes are better at removing loose hairs than others.

Brushing

If your dog is still slightly damp from washing, you can use a shedding rake to dislodge the undercoat. Be careful; if the dog is too damp, the rake may pull on his hair too much and the dog may protest.

More effective than a shedding rake are specially designed de-shedding tools such as the Furminator. These tools push through the outer coat and catch on the undercoat to pull out dead hair. Most of the hair your Aussie sheds is undercoat. These tools are not for removing tangles or mats, and can actually be damaged by using them to attempt to do so. With any shedding tool, don't bear down too hard as you could scratch or bruise your dog's skin.

143

HOME BASICS
Bathing Steps

1. Before washing, brush the dog with a pin brush and remove any tangles or mats, as washing will only make them worse.

2. Mix up a solution of shampoo and water. The shampoo will go a lot further that way.

3. Adjust the water temperature so it would be comfortable for you to bathe in, or just a little cooler. Remember, warmer water loosens hair. Keep checking it throughout.

4. If possible, use a handheld sprayer. One with a massage setting will work best.

5. Wet him down, starting behind his ears. Save his face for last. Tip: To prevent your dog from doing a wet dog shake, keep one hand around one ear.

6. Pour or sponge the shampoo mixture on him. Work shampoo into a lather, massaging down to the skin to help loosen dead hair.

7. Rinse thoroughly, starting at the front and top and working toward the rear and bottom. Use a gentle spray on the face and genitals, but a harder spray on the body. Again, this helps loosen dead hair.

8. Apply a small amount of crème rinse. Rinse again.

9. As soon as you let him go, he'll start running and rolling, so keep him away from dirt!

10. Towel dry him as much as possible.

11. Use a blow-dryer to accelerate drying. A forced-air dryer, which emits cool air at a high velocity, is the best choice because it helps dislodge loose hair.

Shedding in dogs is caused by changes in ambient light levels, not temperature. Because most dogs live indoors and are exposed to artificial lighting, they tend to shed all year round. But they also usually have periods of higher shedding in the spring and fall. Shedding can also increase following a female's season or whelping of puppies, following an illness or fever, or when the dog is nervous—which is one reason why the dog you thought you'd just groomed is suddenly shedding all over the place when you go to the veterinarian. A poor diet can also increase shedding.

When your dog isn't shedding so much, you can just brush him with a pin brush. In winter or in dry climates, spritzing the coat with water or a coat dressing with just a tad of crème rinse (1 tablespoon conditioner to 16 ounces of water) in it will prevent static electricity in the coat. Brush with the growth of the hair at first, making sure to reach all the way down to the skin. You can brush against the growth of the hair afterward, which will loosen dead hairs.

Mats and tangles are more likely to form in the thick hair of the britches, and perhaps behind the ears in some dogs. Rather than cut them out, pull them apart lengthwise as best you can until you can brush them out. A slicker brush is good for this.

Allergies and Parasites

If your Aussie is scratching, chewing, rubbing, and licking he may have allergies, perhaps to inhaled allergens, food, or fleas. The most common inhaled allergens are dander, pollen, dust, and mold. They are often seasonal. Signs most commonly appear between 1 and 3 years of age. Unlike in humans, where hay fever and other inhaled allergens typically cause sneezing, in dogs they more often cause itching. Food, too, can cause allergies. Signs of allergies are typically reddened itchy skin, particularly around the ears, eyes, feet, forelegs, armpits, and abdomen. The dog may scratch and lick, and rub his torso or rump on furniture or rugs.

Breed Needs

Trimming

The Aussie coat should be kept in its natural state, but some neatening is allowed, particularly if you plan to enter the show ring with him. You can use thinning shears to neaten the areas behind and in front of the ears, and to clean up any scraggly hairs on the ears. You can also use thinning shears to shape the tail nub so it disappears into the rump hair. Finally, you can brush the hair on the rear hocks up and use thinning shears to shape it into a straight line, and brush the hair on the toes upward to shape the feet in a clean-looking round shape. None of these steps is necessary for your Aussie at home, however.

The one type of trimming you may want to do is trimming the foot hair. Excess foot hair can carry in additional dirt and mud. Use scissors to carefully cut away long hair that protrudes beyond the foot pads.

FYI: Flea Treatments

Ingredient	Application	Action
Imidacloprid	spot-on, 1–3 months	kills 98% of fleas in 1 hour; continues for 1 month
Fipronil	spray, spot-on, 1–3 months	kills fleas and, to a lesser extent, ticks for 1–3 months
Lufenuron	pill, monthly	renders fleas that bite the dog sterile
Pyriproxyfen	spray, every 3 months	renders fleas that bite the dog sterile
Selamectin	spot-on, monthly	kills and sterilizes fleas; prevents heartworms
Nitenpyram	pill, as needed	instantly kills fleas; no residual action
Metaflumizone	spot-on, monthly	kills fleas in 48 hours; continues for 1 month
Amitraz	spot-on, collar, monthly	kills ticks for up to 1 month
Permethrin	spray, spot-on, as needed	kills fleas and, to a lesser extent, ticks; no residual action

Allergens can be isolated with a skin test in which small amounts of allergen extracts are injected under the skin, which is then monitored for reactions. Besides avoiding allergens, some treatments are available, including antihistamines, glucocorticoids, and hyposensitization.

The most common allergy among all dogs is flea allergy dermatitis (FAD), which is an allergic reaction to the saliva that a flea injects under the skin whenever it feeds. It causes intense itching in the bite area as well as all over the dog, especially around the rump, legs, and paws. Even a single flea bite can cause severe reactions in allergic dogs. The cure? Get rid of fleas.

External Parasites

Fighting fleas used to mean treating your dog, his bedding, your house, and your yard, along with daily vacuuming and flea combing. Now dog owners have options that are easy and effective. Look for products that contain one of the ingredients in the "Flea Treatments" sidebar.

The best course of action is to vary the type of flea product you use, so that fleas have less chance of becoming resistant. For example, use imidacloprid one month, fipronil another, and metaflumizone another. You can also use them in conjunction with lufenuron to prevent fleas from reproducing. Most of these products are available only from your veterinarian, and they cost much more than the traditional flea sprays you can buy in the grocery store. But they're worth it. They're safer and more effective, and because they have residual action, you'll spend far less money in the long run.

Ticks, too, are gradually being beaten by newer products. Still, the old-fashioned ways are worth knowing. If you're in tick territory, examine your dog in the tick-favored spots: on his ears, neck, withers, and between his toes. If you find one, use a tissue to grasp it as close to the skin as possible, and pull it straight out without twisting or squeezing. If you leave the head in, don't worry; it usually won't cause an infection.

Fleas and ticks not only cause intense itching and scratching, but fleas can cause flea allergy dermatitis and tapeworms, and ticks can cause ehrlichiosis, babesia, and Lyme disease, among others. Your veterinarian can order blood tests if these conditions are suspected.

CAUTION

Lyme Disease

A vaccination is available for Lyme disease, but it's not advisable for dogs that don't live in Lyme endemic areas and, in fact, may not even be advisable for those that do live in such areas. Consult your veterinarian.

Mites

Mites can also cause problems. Sarcoptic mites cause sarcoptic mange, an intensely itchy disorder that you can catch. It's often characterized by small bumps and crusts on the ear tips, abdomen, elbows, and hocks. The condition can be treated with repeated shampoos or with an injection.

Demodex mites cause demodectic mange, a noncontagious but often difficult-to-treat condition. A couple of small patches in a puppy are commonplace and will usually go away on their own, but many such patches or a generalized condition must be treated with repeated dips or with drug therapy. Cases involving the feet can be especially difficult to cure.

Ear Care

Like that of all dogs, the Aussie's ear canal is made up of an initial long, vertical segment with an abrupt right-angle turn before reaching the ear drum. And as in all dogs, this design means that moisture and debris can accumulate in that hidden area and cause problems. Ear problems are often signaled by head tilt, head shaking, scratching, inflammation, discharge, debris, or even circling to one side. They can be caused by infections, allergies, seborrhea, foreign bodies, or ear mites.

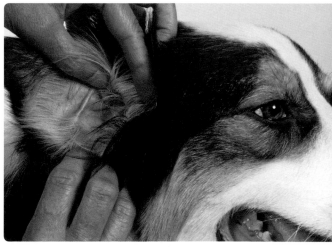

Ear mites are especially common in youngsters. They're contagious, so separate a dog you suspect of having them from other pets. Signs are head shaking, head tilt, and a dark, coffee ground-like buildup in the ears. They itch like mad, so you need to get right to them. Your veterinarian can prescribe ear drops or newer drug therapies.

More harm is done by overzealous cleaning than by no cleaning at all. But if your Aussie has gobs of debris, clean it using an ear cleanser from your veterinarian. Go outdoors, quickly squeeze the cleaner in the ear canal, and gently massage the liquid downward and squish it around. Then stand back and let him shake his head, flinging the sludge all over the place (that's why you're outside). Don't try this if the ear is red, swollen, or painful; these signs call for veterinary attention.

Nail Care

Nails that grow too long impact the ground with every step, displacing the normal position of the toes and causing discomfort, splaying, and even lameness. If dewclaws, those rudimentary "thumbs" on the wrists, are present, they are especially prone to getting caught on things and ripped out, and can even grow in a loop and back into the leg. You need to cut your Aussie's nails at least once a month, and even more often if your dog is less active and the nails aren't worn down as much. The rear nails usually wear more than the front nails, so you may be able to skip cutting the rear nails if your dog is active.

Use nail clippers—the guillotine type are usually easier—and be sure they are sharp. Dull clippers crush the nail and hurt the dog. You can also use a nail grinder, but don't let the heat build up. It's easiest to bend the leg toward the rear of the dog, like a blacksmith works on a horse's hoof. This allows you to see the bottom of the nails and makes it easier to spot the quick, the sensitive and potentially bleeding part of the nail. If you look under the nail you can see where it begins to get hollow; anywhere it looks hollow is quickless. In this same area, the nail will suddenly get much thinner. Again, where it's thin it is safe to cut. In a light-colored nail you can see a redder area that indicates the blood supply; the sensitive quick extends slightly farther down the nail than the blood supply. When in doubt, cut too little and gradually whittle your way higher. You'll eventually goof up and cut the quick. That calls for styptic powder to quell the bleeding and lots of extra treats to assuage your guilt!

Dental Care

Dental care begins in puppyhood, as you teach your Aussie to enjoy getting his teeth brushed. You can start by rubbing your fingers, along with some meat-flavored doggy toothpaste, along his teeth. Work up to a finger brush

Breed Truths

Occlusion

Aussies shed their baby (deciduous) teeth between 4 and 7 months of age. Sometimes the permanent canine teeth will grow in alongside the deciduous canine teeth before the latter are shed. If the two coexist for more than a week, ask your veterinarian if the deciduous teeth may have to be extracted. Otherwise they could displace the permanent teeth and affect the occlusion. Some adult Aussies are missing one or more small premolars, which is a fairly common fault in many breeds of dogs. A few Aussies have extra premolars. An Aussie's teeth should meet such that the top front teeth just barely overlap the bottom ones. This is called a scissors bite. Poor occlusion is one of the more common problems seen in Aussies.

- Overbite: the front top teeth are well in front of the bottom ones, so a gap forms between them
- Level bite: the top and bottom front teeth meet tip to tip
- Underbite: the top front teeth are behind the bottom ones
- Wry mouth: the jaw on one side is longer than on the other
- Anterior crossbite: some, but not all, of the front lower teeth are in front of the upper front teeth
- Dropped center incisors: the two center lower front teeth (incisors) are shorter than the others and often slanted forward

and then a soft-bristled doggy toothbrush. Don't use human toothpaste, which has a taste dogs hate. Brush a little, and give a treat. Make it a habit to brush once a day.

If you let plaque build up, it attracts bacteria and minerals, which harden into tartar. It spreads rootward, causing irreversible periodontal disease with tissue, bone, and tooth loss. The bacteria gain an inlet to the bloodstream, where they can cause kidney and heart valve infections. Hard, crunchy foods don't help as much as they were once thought to, although some special foods are designed to scour the dog's teeth when chewed. Regardless, they don't take the place of brushing. If tartar accumulates, your Aussie may need a thorough cleaning under anesthesia.

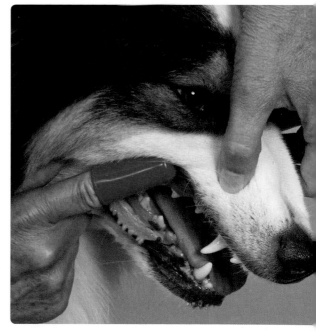

Chapter Nine

The Senior Australian Shepherd

A ussie puppies are fun, and Aussie adults are true companions. But Aussie seniors, with the wisdom of their years, are in many ways the best partners of all. You may need to make some concessions to help them be healthy and comfortable, but the extra effort you put in will be well worth it.

Senior Changes

Older dogs, like older people, may experience sensory or cognitive losses. Fortunately, dogs deal well with these changes—better, in fact, than most people do.

Vision Loss

As your dog ages, you'll start to notice a slight haziness when you look into the pupil (black part) of his eye. That's normal and doesn't affect vision that much. However, if it becomes very gray or even white, he probably has cataracts. A canine ophthalmologist can remove the lens and even replace it with an artificial lens, just like the ones people get. If your Aussie loses his vision, block dangerous places, such as stairways and pools. Don't move your furniture. Place sound and scent beacons around the house and yard so he can hear and smell where he is. Make pathways, such as carpet runners inside and gravel walks outside, so he can feel them with his paws.

Hearing Loss

Older dogs also tend to lose their hearing. The ability to hear high-pitched sounds usually goes first, so try to call out in a lower tone of voice. Aussies can easily learn hand signals, and they can also learn to come to a flashing porch light when out in the yard. Be sure to pet your dog a lot; otherwise he may wonder why you quit talking to him.

Cognitive Loss

If you find your older Aussie walking around aimlessly, pacing back and forth, or standing in a corner looking like he's stuck, he may be suffering from cognitive dysfunction, similar to Alzheimer's in humans. Your veterinarian can prescribe drugs that may help get him back to being his old self. You can also help by involving him in activities and small mental challenges, either through games or by teaching him new tricks. These have been shown to help ward off cognitive impairment.

Senior Health

Your older Aussie should have a veterinary checkup twice a year. Whereas bloodwork may have been optional when he was younger, it's a necessity now. It can tell you if he has kidney failure, diabetes, liver failure, or other problems.

CAUTION

Toenail Time

Don't forget the toenails! Older dogs have tougher nails, and they wear them down less. Toenails can grow to the point that they make walking difficult.

Because the immune system is less effective in older dogs, it's doubly important for you to shield your Aussie from infectious disease. However, if he's turned into a homebody, it may not be necessary for him to continue being vaccinated. As this is an area of controversy, ask your veterinarian about the latest guidelines.

As with people, certain diseases become more likely as dogs age. Kidney disease, heart disease, cancer, and diabetes are among those of greatest concern.

Cancer is a major disease of senior dogs. Warning signs depend on the cancer but can include a new lump, sores, weight loss, lethargy, limping, collapse, and vomiting. Treatment also depends on the type of cancer but may include surgery, chemotherapy, or radiation.

Heart disease is another a major disease of older dogs. Signs include breathing difficulty, coughing, loss of appetite, lethargy, and abdominal distension. A veterinarian can diagnose the condition by listening to the heart and with more extensive tests such as EKG, radiographs, or ultrasound. Treatment may include a special diet and medications.

Arthritis is very common in older dogs. Signs are limping, difficulty getting up, whining, and reluctance to exercise. It can be especially evident after a day of unusual exercise. Your veterinarian can prescribe drugs that may help ease the pain.

Dental problems are also very common in older dogs. Bad breath, bleeding gums, loose teeth, recessed gums, and reluctance to chew are all signs. Your veterinarian can examine your dog's mouth and extract any infected or painful teeth, and may also prescribe medication.

Kidney disease is very common in older dogs. The condition may take months to years to develop, but it usually doesn't show any outward signs until the disease is fairly progressed. Signs include excessive thirst

and urination, weight loss, appetite loss, and vomiting. Your veterinarian can diagnose the condition with urine and blood tests, and may prescribe treatment such as a special diet, medication, and subcutaneous fluids.

Cushing's syndrome, or hyperadrenocorticism, occurs when the body produces too much of the hormone cortisol. Signs include increased hunger, thirst, and urination, as well as lethargy, muscle wasting, hair loss, and especially, a potbellied appearance. Your veterinarian can run urine and blood tests to diagnose the syndrome, and can place your dog on drugs that will help him feel much better.

Helpful Hints

Body Odor

It's not uncommon for older dogs to have a stronger body odor than they did when younger. Search for its source. The most likely sources are the teeth, ear infections, seborrhea, or even kidney disease.

Senior Activities

Even Aussies age, and although they may remain youthful in mind, their bodies often show the toll of their exuberant youth. Foremost among the signs of age are arthritic changes, which may mean you need to tone down the marathon runs or wild disc catches—despite your Aussie's urging to the contrary. Opt for lower impact exercise such as walking and swimming. If he has difficulty getting up and moving around the next day, you may have overdone it.

Just because his body may be slowing doesn't mean his mind is. He still needs mental stimulation. If he enjoys the same games he did when he was younger, great! Just be sure not to overdo them. Try to find some less strenuous games, such as searching for hidden treats, people, or objects, or any game that challenges him to think. Teach new tricks, teach him to track, or simply take him with you for plenty of car rides.

Senior Nutrition

More than 40 percent of dogs between the ages of 5 and 10 years are overweight or obese. And it's not just from less activity or more eating. Changes in metabolic rate cause fewer calories to be burned and more to be stored as fat. A recent study showed that mature dogs require 20 percent fewer calories in order to maintain the same weight as younger ones. Thus, dogs entering old age may benefit from eating a food with less fat and fewer calories.

But there's a catch when it comes to very old dogs. As dogs get very old, they tend to stop gaining weight and instead start losing weight, actually requiring more calories. For these dogs, increasing the fat content of the diet will increase tastiness and calorie content, and also improve protein efficiency.

Older dogs may also have different protein requirements. Even with exercise, older dogs tend to lose muscle mass, which means losses in protein reserves. Losses in muscle tissue and protein reserves may impair the immune system and decrease the body's ability to respond to physical trauma, infectious agents, or stress. To counteract these potential problems, older dogs need higher levels of dietary protein to build and maintain muscle. Contrary to popular opinion, feeding older dogs high-protein diet will not overtax their kidneys—unless the dog already has kidney problems. Dogs with kidney problems need to eat a diet with moderate levels of high-quality protein; however, older dogs without kidney disease can eat a high-protein diet without adverse kidney effects.

In most healthy older dogs, dietary mineral levels can remain the same. For example, sodium restriction is not necessary in older healthy dogs. However, many older dogs are hypertensive or have heart disease. Not only is excess sodium bad for these conditions, but the conditions may also make it difficult to excrete excess sodium in the diet. Most diets supply more sodium than is required, so decreasing sodium is usually a good idea as long as the dog will still eat the food.

CAUTION

Vomiting and Diarrhea

Vomiting or diarrhea can dehydrate and debilitate an old dog quickly. They can also signal some possibly serious problems. So while you may have waited a bit when he was younger, you can't afford to wait and see when it comes to older dogs.

Unlike people, dogs don't seem to suffer from osteoporosis, at least not if they've been maintained on a balanced diet with adequate calcium in earlier years. Thus, senior dogs eating a commercial diet do not need calcium supplementation.

Don't forget the practical aspects. Old dogs are more prone to dehydration, often because of health problems such as kidney disease that cause them to urinate more frequently, or because they're taking medications such as diuretics for heart disease. Making sure the water is fresh, cool, and readily available can help encourage a dog to drink more.

Chapter Ten

The Australian Shepherd Standard

A breed standard is a description of the ideal dog of that breed, describing how the dog should look, move, and act. It is the ideal against which all dogs competing in conformation events are compared. In the United States, Australian Shepherds are judged under two different, but related, standards of perfection. The ASCA, United Kennel Club, and Canadian Kennel Club use the ASCA standard, whereas the AKC uses the AKC standard. Both standards basically seek the same ideal but may sometimes use slightly different wording. As the original standard, the ASCA standard is used here, with any deviations from the AKC standard noted.

Note: *DQ denotes "disqualifying fault," which means a dog with that condition cannot compete in conformation events.*

The ASCA Standard

General Appearance
The Australian Shepherd is a well-balanced dog of medium size and bone. He is attentive and animated, showing strength and stamina, combined with unusual agility. Slightly longer than tall, he has a coat of moderate length and coarseness with coloring that offers variety and individuality in each specimen. An identifying characteristic is the natural or docked bobtail. In each sex, masculinity or femininity is well defined.

AKC note: *The AKC standard also mentions the Aussie's strong herding and guarding instincts. Additionally, it describes the Aussie as lithe, and as being solid and muscular without cloddishness.*

Character
The Australian Shepherd is intelligent, primarily a working dog of strong herding and guardian instincts. He is an exceptional companion. He is versatile and easily trained, performing his assigned tasks with great style and enthusiasm. He is reserved with strangers but does not exhibit shyness. Although an aggressive, authoritative worker, viciousness toward people or animals is intolerable.

AKC note: *The AKC standard emphasizes that any display of shyness, fear, or aggression is to be severely penalized.*

Head

Clean-cut, strong, dry, and in proportion to the body. The top skull is flat to slightly rounded, its length and width each equal to the length of the muzzle, which is in balance and proportioned to the rest of the head. The muzzle tapers slightly to a rounded tip. The stop is moderate but well defined.

AKC note: *The AKC standard states that the muzzle can be slightly shorter than the backskull. Viewed from the side, the topline of the backskull and muzzle form parallel planes divided by the stop. The backskull may show a slight occipital protuberance.*

Teeth

A full complement of strong, white teeth meet in a scissors bite. An even bite is a fault. Teeth broken or missing by accident are not penalized. DQ: undershot bite; overshot bites exceeding $1/8$ inch.

AKC note: *The AKC standard is more tolerant of a level (even) bite but prefers a scissors bite. It also points out that loss of contact of the upper and lower teeth caused by short center incisors in an otherwise correct mouth should not be considered undershot.*

Eyes

Very expressive, showing attentiveness and intelligence. Clear, almond-shaped, and of moderate size, set a little obliquely, neither prominent nor sunken, with pupils dark, well defined, and perfectly positioned. Color is brown, blue, amber, or any variation or combination including flecks and marbling.

AKC note: *The AKC standard does not specify an oblique set, but adds that the expression should be alert and friendly.*

Ears

Set on high at the side of the head, triangular and slightly rounded at the tip, of moderate size with length measured by bringing the tip of the ear around to the inner corner of the eye. The ears, at full attention, break slightly forward and over from one quarter to one half above the base. Prick and hound type ears are severe faults.

AKC note: *The AKC standard does not mention a rounded tip and does not specify length.*

Neck, Topline, Body

The neck is firm, clean, and in proportion to the body. It is of medium length and slightly arched at the crest, settling well into the shoulders. The body is firm and muscular. The topline appears level at a natural four-square stance. The chest is deep and strong with ribs well-sprung. The loin is strong and broad when viewed from the top. The bottom line carries

well back with moderate tuck up. The croup is moderately sloping, the ideal being 30 degrees from the horizontal. Tail is straight, not to exceed 4 inches, natural bobbed or docked.

AKC note: *The AKC standard states that the chest should reach to the elbow.*

Forequarters

The shoulder blades (scapulae) are long and flat, close set at the withers, approximately two fingers' width at a natural stance, and are well laid back at an angle approximating 45 degrees to the ground. The upper arm (humerus) is attached at an approximate right angle to the shoulder line with forelegs dropping straight, perpendicular to the ground. The elbow joint is equidistant from the ground to the withers. The legs are straight and powerful. Pasterns are short, thick, and strong but still flexible, showing a slight angle when viewed from the side. Feet are oval-shaped, compact, with close-knit, well-arched toes. Pads are thick and resilient; nails short and strong. Dewclaws may be removed.

AKC note: *The AKC standard specifies that the bone of the foreleg should be strong, and oval rather than round.*

Hindquarters

Width of hindquarters approximately equal the width of forequarters at the shoulders. The angulation of the pelvis and the upper thigh (femur) corresponds to the angulation of the shoulder blade and upper arm forming an approximate right angle. Stifles are clearly defined, hock joints moderately bent. The metatarsi are short, perpendicular to the ground, and parallel to each other when viewed from the rear. Feet are oval-shaped and compact with close-knit, well-arched toes. Pads are thick and resilient; nails short and strong. Rear dewclaws are removed.

Coat

Of medium texture, straight to slightly wavy, weather-resistant, of moderate length with an undercoat. The quantity of undercoat varies with climate. Hair is short and smooth on the head, outside of ears, front of the forelegs, and below the hocks. Backs of the forelegs are moderately feathered; breeches are moderately full. There is a moderate mane and frill, more pronounced in dogs than bitches. Nontypical coats are severe faults.

Color

All colors are strong, clear, and rich. The recognized colors are blue merle, red (liver) merle, solid black, and solid red (liver), all with or without white markings and/or tan (copper) points with no preference. The blue merle and black have black pigmentation on the nose, lips, and eye-rims. Butterfly nose should not be faulted under 1 year of age. On all colors, the areas surrounding the ears and eyes are dominated by color other than white. The hairline of a white collar does not exceed the point of withers. DQ: other than recognized colors, white body splashes, Dudley nose.

AKC note: The AKC standard more explicitly describes acceptable distribution of white areas. White is acceptable on the neck (but not to exceed the point of withers at the skin), chest, legs, muzzle, underparts, blaze on head, and white extension from underpart up to 4 inches, measured from a horizontal line at the elbow. In addition, white body splashes are defined as white on the body between withers and tail, on the sides between elbows, and the back of hindquarters. It also states that, in merles, it is permissible to have small pink spots on the nose, but that these should not exceed 25 percent of the nose in adults.

Gait

Smooth, free, and easy; exhibiting agility of movement with a well-balanced, ground-covering stride. Fore and hind legs move straight and parallel with the center line of the body; as speed increases, the feet, both front and rear, converge toward the center line of gravity of the dog, while the topline remains firm and level.

AKC note: The AKC standard adds that the dog must be agile and able to change direction or alter gait instantly.

Size

Preferred height at the withers for males is 20 to 23 inches; that for females is 18 to 21 inches; however, quality is not to be sacrificed in favor of size.

Disqualifications

Both the ASCA and AKC disqualify male dogs that are lacking two normally descended testicles, in addition to the disqualifications mentioned within the body of the standard under color and teeth.

Conformation Competition

Do you watch the Westminster dog show and envision you and your Aussie parading around a similar ring? The truth is that unless your Aussie came from a pedigree of show dogs, with Champions (designated by a "Ch" in front of their names) within the first two generations, chances are that he may not have the breeding required to meet the exacting points of the Australian Shepherd standard. If your breeder doesn't compete in dog shows, he or she probably did not choose your dog's parents with an eye toward producing a show dog. If, however, the breeder does compete in shows, ask her whether she thinks your dog is competitive.

For an AKC conformation show, your Aussie cannot have been neutered or spayed, or sold to you with a Limited Registration, all of which will render him ineligible. Only the breeder can change the Limited Registration to Full Registration, so his or her opinion is once again the first one you should seek. ASCA conformation shows offer separate events for neutered or spayed dogs, awarding the Altered Championship (A-Ch) title.

Often, local kennel clubs, which you can locate through the AKC, sponsor conformation handling classes. Here both you and your dog will learn how to behave in the ring. You can practice posing your dog at home by placing his front legs roughly parallel to each other and perpendicular to the ground, and his rear legs also parallel to one another with the hocks (the area from the rear ankle to the foot) perpendicular to the ground. Practice having him trot alertly in a straight line. More important than getting everything perfect is doing it all with a happy attitude. Help him keep this merry outlook through liberal handouts of treats.

Becoming a Champion

At a show, a judge will evaluate your Aussie in regard to type—that is, how well he exemplifies the areas of the standard that define an Aussie as an Aussie, such as head shape, coat, and overall proportions. He will also be evaluated on soundness, his ability to walk or trot in as efficient a manner as possible. Finally he'll be evaluated on temperament, checking that he is neither shy nor aggressive. If he ranks high in comparison to his competition, he may win from 1 to 5 points toward his championship, depending on how many dogs he's defeated. For an AKC championship, a dog must win 15 points, including two major wins (3- to 5-point wins); for an ASCA championship, a dog must win 15 points, including three majors.

Resources

Organizations

Australian Shepherd Club of
America: *www.asca.org*

United States Australian Shepherd
Association:
www.australianshepherds.org

American Kennel Club:
www.akc.org

United Kennel Club:
www.ukcdogs.com

Australian Shepherd Health &
Genetics Institute:
www.ashgi.org

American Herding Breed
Association:
www.ahba-herding.org

Australian Shepherd Trial
Association:
www.a-s-t-a.org

North American Miniature
Australian Shepherd Club
of the USA:
www.namascusa.com

Miniature Australian Shepherd
Club of America:
www.mascaonline.net

Rescue

Aussie Rescue and
Placement Helpline:
www.aussierescue.org

Second Time Around Aussie
Rescue: *www.staar.org*

Petfinder:
www.petfinder.org
(national database of all breeds
in shelters)

Aussie Information

Working Aussie Source:
www.workingaussiesource.com

Aussie Info:
www.aussieinfo.org

Herding on the Web:
www.herdingontheweb.com

Ranch Dog Trainer:
www.ranchdogtrainer.com

Pedigree Database:
www.hrdndog.com/pedigrees

History:
www.lasrocosa.com/aussiehistory.html

Magazines

Australian Shepherd Journal:
www.australianshepherds.org/
journal.html

Aussie Times:
www.asca.org/aussietimes

Double Helix Network News:
www.ashgi.org/reading.htm

Stockdog Journal:
stockdogjournal.com

AKC magazines:
www.akc.org/pubs/index.cfm

Various dog magazines:
www.dogchannel.com

Books

The Australian Shepherd Manual.
P.O. Box 88, Ridgeland, MS 39158

Coile, D. Caroline. *Show Me!*
Hauppauge, NY: Barron's, 1997.

Cornwell, Sandy. *Judging the
Australian Shepherd.* 10346 E 2600
N. Road, Potomac, IL 61865, 1985.

Hartnagle-Taylor, Jeanne Joy. *All About Aussies*. Loveland, CO: Alpine, 1996.

Holland, Vergil S. *Herding Dogs: Progressive Training*. New York: Macmillan, 1994.

Mistretta, Victoria and Christina Mistretta. *The Structure and Movement of the Australian Shepherd*. 3167 Dodge Road, White City, OR 97503

Palika, Liz. *The Australian Shepherd: Champion of Versatility*. New York: Howell, 1995.

Other Resources

Books for sale:
www.lasrocosa.com/education.html
Training DVD:
http://users.htcomp.net/slashv/ trainingyourstockdog.htm
ASCA yearbooks: available through the ASCA

Discussion Groups

www.yahoogroups.com
www.australianshepherds.org/ onlinestuff.htm

Health and Research

AKC Canine Health Foundation
www.akcchf.org

Animal Health Trust
www.aht.org.uk
(*www.aht.org.uk/genetics_tests.html* for cataract DNA test)

Australian Shepherd Health and Genetics Institute
www.ashgi.org

Canine Eye Registration Foundation
www.vmdb.org

Canine Health Information Center
www.caninehealthinfo.org

MDR1 testing
www.vetmed.wsu.edu/depts-VCPL/ test.aspx

Morris Animal Foundation
www.morrisanimalfoundation.org

National Animal Poison Control Center
(800) 548-2423
www.napcc.aspca.org

Optigen (DNA Testing for PRA)
www.optigen.com

Orthopedic Foundation for Animals
www.offa.org

Rescue

Aussie Rescue and Placement Helpline
www.aussierescue.org

Second Time Around Aussie Rescue
www.staar.org

PetFinder
www.petfinder.org

Index

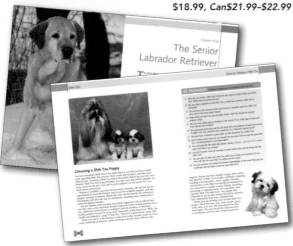

THE TEAM BEHIND THE *TRAIN YOUR DOG* DVD

Host **Nicole Wilde** is a certified Pet Dog Trainer and internationally recognized author and lecturer. Her books include *So You Want to Be a Dog Trainer* and *Help for Your Fearful Dog* (Phantom Publishing). In addition to working with dogs, Nicole has been working with wolves and wolf hybrids for over fifteen years and is considered an expert in the field.

Host **Laura Bourhenne** is a Professional Member of the Association of Pet Dog Trainers, and holds a degree in Exotic Animal Training. She has trained many species of animals including several species of primates, birds of prey, and many more. Laura is striving to enrich the lives of pets by training and educating the people they live with.

Director **Leo Zahn** is an award winning director/cinematographer/editor of television commercials, movies, and documentaries. He has directed and edited more than a dozen instructional DVDs through the Picture Company, a subsidiary of Picture Palace, Inc., based in Los Angeles.